Cosmosophy

Cosmosophy

Volume 1

Eleven Lectures by
Rudolf Steiner
Given in Dornach, September 23–October 16, 1921

Anthroposophic Press

Translated from shorthand reports, unrevised by the lecturer from the German edition published with the title *Anthroposophie als Kosmosophie*, part one (Vol. 207 in the Bibliographical Survey, 1961). Revised translation by Alice Wulsin. Lecture 10 was translated by Michael Klein and edited by Alice Wulsin.

Copyright © 1985
by Anthroposophic Press

Library of Congress Cataloging in Publication Data

Steiner, Rudolf, 1861–1925.
  Cosmosophy: eleven lectures given in Dornach, September 23–October 16, 1921.

  Translation of: Anthroposophie als Kosmosophie.
  1. Anthroposophy—Addresses, essays, lectures.
I. Title.
BP595.S894A5813   1984   299'.935   84-21737
ISBN 0-88010-120-2 (v. 1)
ISBN 0-88010-111-3 (pbk.: v. 1)

Cover: Graphic form by Rudolf Steiner
Title Lettering: Peter Stebbing

All rights reserved. No part of this book may be reproduced in any form without the written permission of the publishers, except for brief quotations embodied in critical articles and reviews.

Contents

Foreword by Alan Howard xi

I. *September 23, 1921*
Eastern and Western civilizations in a spiritual light; love and fear; world-knowledge and self-knowledge; the Western mysteries (Ireland); Bulwer-Lytton and his novel *Zanoni*; the inner nature of the human being as a reflecting apparatus; the source of destruction within the human being as the prerequisite of the independent, thinking human being; the origin of fear in Western civilization; the mystery of evil; the contrasting nature of Eastern and Western blood; the Washington Conference; the comments of General Smuts. 1

II. *September 24, 1921*
Filling the inner source of destruction with moral ideals; the Jupiter existence of the earth; ordinary consciousness as the world of the Father God; Adolf Harnack as the advocate of the Father God; Soloviev's differentiation between the Father God and the Son God; the inner word; the declining and ascending worlds; the rainbow and flesh color; Christianity as the religion of resurrection; the world of the moon and the sun as the world of the Father and the Son; the coming of Christ and man. 18

III. *September 30, 1921*
Foundations of an occult psychology out of Imaginative cognition; sleeping and waking in higher cognition; the world of objective streaming thoughts and of subjective thoughts; feelings as submerged dreams; the will as a sleep-experience, independent of the body; thinking, feeling, and willing in the spaces between the physical body, etheric body, astral body, and I; past and future karma. 36

IV. *October 1, 1921*
Dream consciousness in the animal soul life; plant consciousness in summer and winter; mineral consciousness as consciousness of our deeds; the relationship of the human being to the hierarchies in Imagination, Inspiration, and Intuition; metamorphosis of the worlds of thought and will in the life after death; the human being between the realms of the higher hierarchies and the realms of nature. 52

V. *October 2, 1921*
The thought world in the region of the sense organization; feeling as a subjective entity; Goethe's mood of soul in the year 1790; the meeting of past and future in the mood of soul; the will as a battlefield of moral ideals with human instincts and drives; the preparation of the future out of the nature of the will; the conscience; cosmic cold and earthly warmth in the constitution of the human being. 71

VI. *October 7, 1921*
Anthroposophy as cosmosophy; the spirit of the human being and life after death; coloring the mineral consciousness by moral feeling; the relationship of the human being to angel and archangel (folk-spirit); appearance of plant consciousness in the Midnight Hour of Existence; descent through animal consciousness in the realm of the archai; the Zodiac; the human being as the experienced environment; entrance into the planetary spheres; the soul-permeation of the animal organization; the significance of the soul-spiritual environment; self-knowledge and world-knowledge. 88

VII. *October 8, 1921*
The human being in life after death; mineral consciousness and plant consciousness; characterization of Goethe in relation to Shakespeare; animal consciousness; the relationship of the human being to the group-souls of the animals and organ-formation; preparation of the etheric body in the planetary world; the earthly germ as chaos; astral fruit of the earth and etheric-cosmic fruit; the influence of karma; the in-breathing and outbreathing of the cosmos in the human being. 107

VIII. *October 9, 1921*
The past of higher entities and the spirit of the human being; the mineral-plant realm and the plant-animal realm as realms of nature in the future; the animal-human realm; the human-soul realm; the manifestation of the inner being of man in the outer physical element on

the Jupiter planet; Friedrich Nietzsche and "superman"; the bodily members of man as seeds for future worlds; world past and earthly future. 122

IX. *October 14, 1921*
Spiritual scientific presentation of today's intellectual human being; spiritual science as the bestower of life forces; quoting and characterizing a present-day human being (Gottfried Benn) and the necessity of spiritual science for him. 136

X. *October 15, 1921*
Dull, I-like life of will and waking thought shadow-pictures; the awakening of the dull I through the appearance of the senses; union with the dead through concrete mental images not through abstract thoughts; reversal of sense experience in the life after death; the philosopher, Feuerbach, and his teachings; Richard Wagner; the totality of sense perceptions: warmth, light, chemical workings, life; refutation of relativity; the problem of spiritual weight; the loss of one's own being in intellectualism and regaining it in deeds out of pure thinking. 145

XI. *October 16, 1921*
Viewing the Mystery of Golgotha in the age of freedom; the appearance of the senses as prerequisite for freedom; the modern human being's lack of freedom in the life after death; overcoming this through the experience of freedom in earthly life; the modern world pic-

ture without beginning and end; the earlier world picture between cosmogony and Last Judgment; Rotteck's *World History*; the senselessness of modern history; Arthur Schopenhauer; the Mystery of Golgotha as the sense-giving center to historical events; spiritual science and the evangelists; Christ as spirit sun being; Overbeck and modern theology. 163

Notes 179

Foreword

This is one of many courses of lectures given by Rudolf Steiner (1861-1925) in the early years of this century, in the amplification of his *spiritual science* or *anthroposophy*. Some of these courses were given to members of the Anthroposophical Society who had been familiar with the subject for many years. Others were given to the general public. In both cases—and naturally more particularly and esoterically so in the former—they were a deepening and extension of what was contained in his written works.

It is the written works that contain the essentials of his teaching. Among them are some which have come to be known as the "basic books," and without some knowledge of them it is impossible to appreciate what was spoken of in these lecture courses. Those basic books are: *The Philosophy of Freedom* (also published as *The Philosophy of Spiritual Activity*), *Theosophy, An Outline of Occult Science, Knowledge of the Higher Worlds and Its Attainment,* and *Christianity as Mystical Fact* (also published as *Christianity and Occult Mysteries of Antiquity*).

It is essential to make this clear to readers, and even to impress upon them the need to have some familiarity with the basic books before attempting the courses. The reasons should be obvious. First, it would be unfair to the readers themselves to be led into buying a book which they might find mystifying and confusing, if not wholly incomprehensible, later; and secondly, and perhaps more importantly, it would be unfair to the cause of spiritual science if the unadvised reader should be led to forming a premature judgment about what is admittedly recondite, if not at times arcane, through insufficient knowledge of its basic principles.

Any scientific investigation—and anthroposophy is just that, even though its field is the supersensible—presupposes a discipline which demands a thorough grounding in its fundamentals. This was all Rudolf Steiner ever asked for the results of his investigations, which he gave out in these and other lectures. So finally, it would be unfair to his unchallenged reputation as a scholar and philosopher to offer to the public such a book as this without these few introductory remarks.

Alan Howard

I

Dornach, September 23, 1921

If an Oriental sage of ancient times—we must return to very ancient times of Oriental culture if we are to consider what I wish to say here—one who had been initiated into the mysteries of the ancient East, were to turn his gaze on modern Western civilization, he might say to its representatives, "You are really living entirely in fear; your whole mood of soul is governed by fear. Everything you do, but also everything you feel, is saturated with fear and its reverberations in the most important moments of life. Since fear is closely related to hatred, hatred plays a great role in your entire civilization."

Let us make this quite clear. I mean that a sage of the ancient Eastern civilization would speak in this way if he stood again today among Western people with the same standard of education, the same mood of soul, as those of his ancient time. He would make it plain that in his time and his country, civilization was founded on a completely different basis. He would probably say, "In my day, fear played no part in civilized life. Whenever we were to promulgate a world conception, allowing action and social life to spring from it, the main thing was joy—joy that could be enhanced to the point of a complete giving of oneself to the world, that then could be enhanced to love." This is how he would experience it, and he would indicate as a result (if he were rightly understood) what were from his point of view the most important ingredients, the most important impulses, of modern civilization. If we knew how to listen to him in the right way, we would gain much that we really need to know in order to find a starting point for trying to get a grip on modern life. Actually, an echo of the ancient civilization still prevails in Asia, though strong European influences have been absorbed into its religious, aesthetic, scientific, and social life. This ancient civilization is in decline, and when the ancient Oriental sage says, "Love was the fundamental force of the ancient Oriental civilization," then certainly it must be admitted that but little of this love can be traced directly in the present. One who is able to discern it, however, can see even now, in the phenomena of decline of the Asiatic culture, the penetration of this primeval element of joy, of delight in the world and love for the world.

In those ancient times there was in the Orient little of what afterward has been required of man since the thought resounded that found its most radical expression in the Greek saying, "Know thyself!" This "Know thyself" actually entered human historical life only in the ancient Greek culture. The ancient Eastern world conception, comprehensive and light-filled, was not yet permeated by this kind of human knowledge; it was in no way oriented toward directing man's gaze into his own being.

In this respect the human being is dependent on the conditions prevailing in his environment. The ancient Oriental culture was founded under a different effect of sunlight on the earth, and its earthly conditions were also different from those of the later Western culture. In the ancient East, man's inner gaze was captured, one could say, by all that surrounds the human being as the world, and he had a special inducement for giving over his entire inner being to the world. It was cosmic knowledge that blossomed in the ancient Oriental wisdom and in the view of the world that owed its origin to this wisdom. Even in the mysteries themselves—you can infer this from all you have been hearing for many years—in all that lived in the mysteries of the East there was no actual adherence to the challenge, "Know thyself!" On the contrary—"Turn your gaze outward toward the world and try to let that approach you which is hidden in the depths of cosmic phenomena!"—that is how the challenge of the ancient Oriental culture would have been expressed.

The teachers and pupils of the mysteries were compelled, however, to turn their gaze to the inner being of man when the Asiatic civilization began to spread westward. As soon, indeed, as mystery colonies were founded in Egypt and in North Africa, but particularly when the mysteries began to develop their colonies still further to the West—a special center was ancient Ireland—then the teachers and pupils of the mysteries coming over from Asia were faced, simply by virtue of the geographical conditions of the Western world and its entirely different elemental configuration, with the necessity of cultivating self-knowledge and a true inner vision. Simply because these mystery pupils, when still in Asia, had acquired knowledge of the outer world—knowledge of the spiritual facts and beings lying behind the outer world—simply through this, they were now able to penetrate deeply into all that actually exists in man's innermost being. In Asia all this could not have been observed at all. The inward-turning gaze would have been paralyzed, so to speak. By means of all that was brought from the East to the Western mystery colonies, however, man's gaze having long been directed outward so as to penetrate into the spiritual worlds, was now enabled to penetrate into man's inner being. It was actually only the strongest souls who could endure what they perceived. Man's inner being actually first came to the consciousness of humanity in these mystery colonies transported from the Orient and founded in Western regions.

One can indeed realize what an impression was produced by this self-knowledge on the teachers and pupils of the Oriental mysteries if we repeat a saying that was addressed to the pupils over and over again by the teachers who had already cultivated that vision of man's inner being, a saying that was to make clear to them in what kind of mood of soul this self-knowledge was actually to be approached. The saying to which I am referring is frequently quoted. In its full weight it was uttered only in the more ancient mystery colonies of Egypt, North Africa, and Ireland as a preparation for the pupil and as a reminder for every initiate regarding the experiences of man's inner being. The saying runs thus, "No one who is not initiated in the sacred mysteries should discover the secrets of man's inner being; to utter these secrets in the presence of a non-initiate is forbidden; the mouth uttering these secrets lays the burden of sin upon itself, and the ear burdens itself with sin when it hearkens to those secrets."

Time and again this saying was uttered from the inner experience that an individual, prepared by Oriental wisdom, was able to attain when he penetrated, by virtue of the earthly conditions of the West, to knowledge of the human being. Tradition has preserved this saying, and today it is still repeated—without any understanding of its innermost nature—in the secret orders and secret societies of the West that outwardly still have a great influence. It is repeated only from tradition, however. It is not uttered with the necessary weight, for those who say it do not really know what it signifies. Even in our time, however, this saying is used as a kind of motto in the secret orders of the West: "There are secrets concerning man's inner being that can be transmitted to people only within the secret societies, for otherwise the mouth uttering them is sinful, and the ear hearing them is likewise sinful."

One must say that, as time has evolved, many people—not in Central Europe but in Western lands—learn in their secret societies what has been handed down as tradition from the researches of the ancient wisdom. It is received without understanding, although as an impulse it actually often flows into action. In more recent centuries, actually since the middle of the fifteenth century, the human constitution has become such as to make it impossible to see these things in their original form; they could be absorbed only intellectually. One could receive concepts about them, but one could not attain a true experience of them. Individuals had only some intimations of it. Many people could penetrate into this realm of experience through such intimations.

Such people have sometimes adopted strange forms of outer life, as, for instance, Bulwer Lytton, who wrote *Zanoni*.[1] What he became in his later life can be grasped only if one knows how he received, to begin with, the tradition of self-knowledge, but how, by virtue of his particular, individual constitution, he was also able to penetrate into certain mysteries. He thereby became estranged from the natural ways of life. Precisely in him it is possible to see what a man's attitude toward life becomes when he admits into his inner experience this "foreign" spiritual world, not merely into his concepts but into his whole mood of soul. Many facts must then be judged by other than conventional standards.

It appeared, of course, quite outlandish when Bulwer traveled about, speaking of his inner experiences with a certain emphasis, while a young woman who accompanied him played a harp-like instrument, for he always needed to have this harp-music in between the passages of his talk. Here and there he appeared in gatherings where everything else went on in a completely formal, conventional way. He would enter in his rather eccentric garb and sit down, with his harp-maiden seated in front of his knees. He would speak a few sentences; then the harp-maiden would play; then he would continue his talk, and the maiden would play again. Something coquettish, in a higher sense of the word —one cannot help characterizing it in this way at first—was thus introduced into the ordinary world where pedantic human convention has made such increasing inroads, particularly since the middle of the fifteenth century.

Humanity has little idea of the degree of conventionalism into which it has grown; people have less and less idea of it simply because it comes to seem natural. One sees something as reasonable only insofar as it is in line with what is "done." Things in life, however, are all interconnected, and the dryness and indolence of modern times, the relationship human beings now have to one another, belongs to the intellectual development of the last few centuries. The two things belong together. A man such as Bulwer Lytton, of course, did not fit into such a development; one can quite well picture to oneself people of more ancient times traveling about in the world accompanied by a younger person with some pleasant music. The disparity between one attitude of soul and another need only be seen in the right light; then such a thing can be understood. With Bulwer Lytton, however, something lit up in him that no longer could exist directly in the modern intellectual age but only as tradition.

One must, however, recover the knowledge of the human being that lived in the mystery colonies of which I have spoken. The ordinary human being today is aware of the world around him by means of his outer, physical sense impressions. What he sees, he orders and arranges with his intellect. Then he looks also into his own inner being. Basically this is the world that man surveys and out of which he acts. The sense impressions received from outside, the mental images developed from these sense impressions, these mental images as they penetrate within, becoming transformed by impulses of feeling and of will, together with everything that is reflected back into consciousness as memories—here we have what forms the content of the soul, the content of life in which modern man weaves and out of which he acts. At most modern man is led by a kind of false mysticism to ask, "What is actually within my inner being? What does self-knowledge yield?" In raising such questions he wishes to find the answer in his ordinary consciousness. This ordinary consciousness, however, only emerges from what actually originated in outer sense impressions and has been transformed by feeling and will. One finds only the reflections, the mirror-images, of outer life when looking into one's inner being with ordinary consciousness; and although the outer impressions are transformed by feeling and will, man still does not know how feeling and will actually work. For this reason he often fails to recognize what he sees in his inner being as a transformed mirror-image of the outer world and takes it, perhaps, as a special message from the divine, eternal world. This is not the case, however. What appears to the ordinary consciousness of modern man as self-knowledge is only the transformed outer world, which is reflected out of man's inner being into his consciousness.

If man really wished to look into his inner being, he would be obliged—I have often used this image—to break the inner mirror. Our inner being is indeed like a mirror. We gaze on the outer world. Here are the outer sense impressions. We link mental images to them. These mental images are then reflected by our inner being. By looking into our inner being we arrive only at this mirror (see drawing, red). We see what is reflected in this memory mirror (red arrows). We are just as unable to gaze into man's inner being with ordinary consciousness as we are to look behind a mirror without breaking it. This, however, is precisely what was brought about in the preparatory stage of the ancient path of Oriental wisdom: the teachers and pupils of the mystery centers that came to the West could penetrate directly through the memories into the inner being of man. Out of what they discovered they afterward spoke those words that actually were meant to convey that one had to be

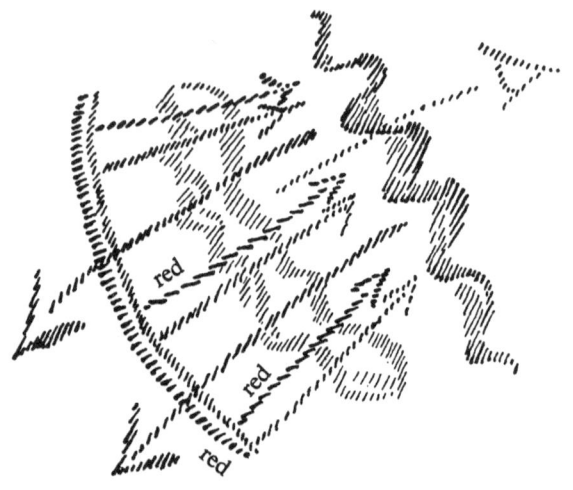

well prepared—above all in those ancient times—if one wished to direct one's gaze to the inner being of man.

What, then, does one behold within the human being? There, one sees how something of the power of perceiving and thinking, which is developed in front of the memory-mirror, penetrates below this memory-mirror. Thoughts penetrate below this memory-mirror and work into the human etheric body, into that part of the etheric body that forms the basis of growth but is also the origin of the forces of will. In looking out into the sunlit space and surveying all that we receive through our sense impressions, there radiates into our inner being something that on the one hand becomes memory images but that also trickles through the memory-mirror, permeating it just as the processes of growth, nutrition, and so on permeate us.

The thought-forces first permeate the etheric body, and the etheric body, permeated in this way by the thought-forces, works in quite a special way on the physical body. Thereupon a complete transformation arises of the material existence that is within the physical body of man. In the outer world, matter is nowhere completely destroyed. This is why modern philosophy and science speak of the conservation of matter, but this law of the conservation of matter is valid only for the outer world. Within the human being, matter is completely dissolved into nothingness. The very essence of matter is fully destroyed. It is precisely upon this fact that our human nature is based: upon being able to throw back matter into chaos, to destroy matter utterly, within that sphere that lies deeper than memory.

This is what was pointed out to the mystery pupils who were led from the East into the mystery colonies of the West, especially Ireland. "In your inner being, below the capacity for memory, you bear within you something that works destructively, and without it you could not have developed your thinking, for you must develop thinking by permeating the etheric body with thought-forces. An etheric body that is permeated with thought-forces, however, works on the physical body in such a way as to throw its matter back into chaos and to destroy it." If, therefore, a person ventures into this inner being of man with the same attitude with which he penetrates as far as memory, he enters a realm where the being of man wants to destroy, to extinguish, what is there. For the purpose of developing the human, thought-filled "I" or ego, we all bear within us, below the memory-mirror, a fury of destruction, a fury of dissolution, in relation to matter. There is no self-knowledge that does not point with the greatest intensity toward this inner human fact.

For this reason, whoever has had to learn of the presence of this source of destruction[2] in the inner being of man must take an interest in the evolution of the spirit. With all intensity he must be able to say to himself: spirit must exist and, for the sake of the continuance of the spirit, matter should be extinguished.

It is only after humanity has been spoken to for many years about the interests connected with spiritual scientific investigation that attention can be drawn to what actually exists within the human being. Today we *must* do so, however, for otherwise man would consider himself to be something different from what he really is within Western civilization. Within Western civilization man is the sheath for a source of destruction, and actually the forces of decline can be transformed into forces of ascent only if man becomes conscious of this, that he is the sheath for a source of destruction.

What would happen if man were not to be led by spiritual science out of this consciousness? Already in the evolution of our time we can see what would happen. What is isolated, separated, as it were, in the human being, and should work only *within* him, at the single spot within where matter is thrown back into chaos, now breaks out and penetrates outer human instincts. That is what will happen to Western civilization, yes, and to the civilization of the whole earth. This is shown by all the destructive forces appearing today—in Eastern Europe, for instance. It is a fury of destruction thrust out of the inner being of man into the outer world, and in the future man will be able to find his bearings regarding what actually flows into his instincts only when a true knowledge of the human being once again prevails, when we become aware once more of the human source of destruction within, which *must* be there, however, for the sake of the evolution of human thinking. This strength of thinking that man must have in order that he may have a world conception in keeping with our time, this strength of thinking which must be there in front of the memory-mirror, brings about the continuation of thinking into the etheric body, and the etheric body thus permeated by thinking works destructively upon the physical body. This source of destruction within modern Western man is a fact, and knowledge merely draws attention to it. If the source of destruction is there without man being able to bring it to consciousness, it is much worse than if man takes full cognizance of this source of destruction and from this standpoint enters into the evolution of modern civilization.

When the pupils of these mystery colonies, of which I have spoken, first heard of these secrets, their immediate response was fear. This fear they learned to know thoroughly. They became thoroughly acquainted with the sensation that a penetration into man's inner being—not frivolously in the sense of a nebulous mysticism but undertaken in all sincerity—must instill fear. This fear felt by the ancient mystery pupils of the West was overcome only by disclosing to them the whole significance of the facts. Then they were able to conquer through consciousness what had to arise in them as fear.

When the age of intellectualism set in, this same fear became unconscious, and as unconscious fear it is still active. Under all kinds of masks it works into outer life. It is suited to the modern age, however, to penetrate into man's inner being. "Know thyself" has become a rightful demand. It was by a deliberate calling forth of fear, followed by an overcoming of this fear, that the mystery pupils were directed to self-knowlege in the right way.

The age of intellectualism dulled the sight of what lay in man's inner being, but it was unable to do away with the fear. It thus came about that man was and still is under the influence of this unconscious fear to the degree of saying, "There is nothing at all in the human being that transcends birth and death." He is afraid of penetrating deeper than this life of memory, this ordinary life of thought, which maintains its legitimacy, after all, only between birth and death. He is afraid to look down into what is actually eternal in the human soul, and from this fear he postulates the doctrine that there is nothing at all outside this life between birth and death. Modern materialism has arisen out of fear, without having the least intimation of this. The modern materialistic world conception is a product of fear and anxiety.

This fear thus lives on in the outer actions of human beings, in the social structure, in the course of history since the middle of the fifteenth century, and especially in the nineteenth century materialistic world conception. Why did these people become materialists, that is, why would they admit only the outer, that which is given in material existence? Because they were afraid to descend into the depths of the human being.

This is what the ancient Oriental sage would have wished to express from his knowledge by saying, "You modern Westerners live entirely steeped in fear. You establish your social order upon fear; you create your arts out of fear; your materialistic world conception has been born from fear. You and the successors of those who in my time established the ancient Oriental world conception, although they have come into decadence now—you and these people of Asia will never understand one another, because with the Asiatic people, after all, everything sprang ultimately from love; with you everything originates in fear mixed with hate."

This certainly sounds radical, so I prefer to try to bring the facts before you as an utterance from the lips of an ancient Oriental sage. It will perhaps be believed that such a one could speak in this way were he to return, whereas a modern person might be considered foolish if he put these things so radically! From such a radical characterization of these things, however, we can learn what we really must learn today for the healthy progress of civilization. Humanity will have to know again that rational thinking, which is the highest attainment of modern times, could not have come into existence if the life of ideas did not arise from a source of destruction. This source must be recognized, so that it may be kept safely within and not pass over into outer instincts and thence become a social impulse.

One can really penetrate deeply into the connections of

modern life by looking at things in this way. The world that manifests as a source of destruction lies within, beyond the memory-mirror. The life of modern man, however, takes its course between the memory-mirror and the outer sense perceptions. Just as little as the human being, when he looks into his inner being, is able to see beyond the memory-mirror, so far is he from being able to penetrate through all that is spread out before him as sense perception; he cannot see beyond it. He adds to it a material, atomistic world, which is indeed a fantastic world, because he cannot penetrate through the sensory mental images.

Man is no stranger, however, to this world beyond the outer, sensory mental images. Every night between falling asleep and awakening he penetrates this world. When you sleep, you dwell within this world. What you experience there beyond the sensory mental images is not the atomistic world conjectured by the visionaries of natural science. What lies beyond the sphere of the senses was actually experienced by the ancient Oriental sage in his mysteries. One can experience it, however, only when one has devotion for the world, when one has the desire and the urge to surrender oneself entirely to the world. Love must hold sway in cognition if one wishes to penetrate beyond the sense impression. It was this love in cognition that prevailed especially in the ancient Oriental civilization.

Why must one have this devotion? One must have this devotion because, if one sought to enter the world beyond the senses with one's ordinary human I, one would be harmed. The I, as experienced in ordinary life, must be given up if one wishes to penetrate into the world beyond the senses. How does this I originate? This I is formed by the human being's capacity to plunge into the chaos of destruction. This I must be forged and hardened in that world lying within man as a source of destruction. With this I one cannot live beyond the sphere of the outer sense world.

Let us picture to ourselves the source of destruction in

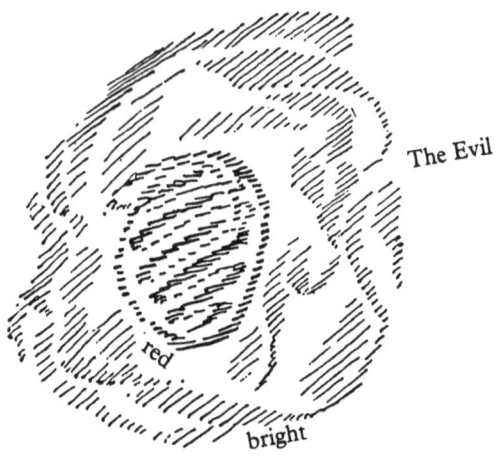

man's inner being (see drawing, red). It extends over the whole human organism. What I am portraying is to be understood intensively, not extensively, but I would like to sketch it for you. Here is the source of destruction, here the human sheath. If what is inside were to spread out over the whole world, what would then live in the world through man? Evil! Evil is nothing but the chaos thrust outside, the chaos that is necessary in man's inner being. In this chaos, which must be within man, this necessary source of evil in man, the human I, the human egoity, must be forged. This human egoity cannot live beyond the sphere of the human senses in the outer world. That is why the I-consciousness disappears in sleep, and when it figures in dreams it often appears as though estranged or weakened.

The I, which is actually forged in the source of evil, cannot pass beyond the sphere of the sense phenomena. Hence to the perception of the ancient Oriental sage it was clear that one can go further only through devotion, through love, through a surrender of the I—and that on penetrating fully into this further region one is no longer in a world of

Vana, of the weaving in the habitual, but rather in the world of Nirvana, where this habitual existence is dispersed.

This interpretation of Nirvana, of the sublimest surrender of the I, as it exists in sleep, as it existed in fully conscious cognition for the pupils of the ancient Oriental civilization—it is this Nirvana that would be alluded to by an ancient Oriental such as the one I introduced to you hypothetically. He would say, "With you, since you had to cultivate the egoity, everything is founded on fear. With us, who had to suppress the ego, everything was founded on love. With you, there speaks the I that desires to assert itself. With us, Nirvana spoke, while the I flowed out lovingly into the entire world."

One can formulate these matters in concepts, and they are then preserved in a certain way, but for humanity they live as sensations, as feelings, fluctuating and permeating human existence. Such feelings and sensations constitute what lives today on the one hand in the Orient and on the other in the West. In the West, human beings have a blood, they have a lymph, that is saturated by egoity forged in the inner source of evil. In the Orient, human beings have a blood, a lymph, in which lives an echo of the longing for Nirvana.

Both in the East and in the West these things escape the crude intellectual concepts of our time. Intellectual understanding strives somehow to draw the blood from the living organism, put it on a slide, place it under a microscope, look at it, and then form ideas about it. The ideas thus arrived at are infinitely crude, even from the point of view of ordinary experience. This is all that can be said. Do you believe that this method touches the subtly graded distinctions between the people who sit here next to one another? The microscope naturally gives only crude concepts about the blood, about the lymph. Subtle shades of difference are to be found even among people who have come from the same milieu. These nuances, however, naturally exist much more intensely between human beings of the East and those of the West, although only a crude picture of them can be gained by the modern intellect.

All this thus lives in the bodies of the human being from Asia, Europe, and America, and in their relation to one another in outer social life. With the crude intellect that has been applied in the last few centuries to the investigation of outer nature, we shall not be able to tackle the demands of modern social life; above all we shall not be able to find the balance between East and West, though this balance must be found.

In the late autumn of this year (1921) people will be going to the Washington Conference,[3] and discussions will take place there about matters that were summed up by General Smuts,[4] England's Minister of South Africa, with, I would say, an instinctive genius. The evolution of modern humanity, he said, is characterized by the fact that the starting point for cultural interests, which has hitherto been in the regions bordering the North Sea and the Atlantic Ocean, is now moving to the Pacific. The culture of the regions situated around the North Sea has gradually spread throughout the West and will become a world culture. The center of gravity of this world culture will be transferred from the North Sea to the Pacific.

Humanity stands face to face with this change. People still talk, however, in such a way that their speech emerges out of the old, crude concepts, and nothing essential is reached—although it must be reached if we are really to move forward. The signs of the times stand with menacing significance before us, and they say to us: until now only a limited trust has been needed between human beings, who in fact were all secretly afraid of one another. This fear was masked under all sorts of other feelings. Now, however, we need an attitude of soul that will be able to embrace a world culture. We need a trust that will be able to bring into balance the contrasts of East and West. Here a significant perspective opens up, which we need. People today believe that economic problems can be handled quite on their own account—the future position of Japan in the Pacific, or how to provide all the trading peoples on earth with free access to the Chinese market, and so on. These problems, however, will not be settled at any conference until people become aware that all economic activities and relations presuppose the trust of one human being in another. In the future this trust can be attained only in a spiritual way. Outer culture will be in need of spiritual deepening. I wished today to look from a different viewpoint at matters we have discussed often before. Tomorrow we shall speak further in this way.

II

Dornach, September 24, 1921

Yesterday I spoke of how we find within the human being a kind of source of destruction. I showed that as long as we remain within ordinary consciousness we retain memories only of the impressions of the world. We gain experience of the world, and we have our experiences through the senses, through the intellect, through the effects generally upon our life of soul. Later we are able to call up again our memory of the afterimage of what we have experienced. We carry as our inner life these afterimages of sense experiences.

It is indeed as though we had within us a mirror, but one that works differently from the ordinary spatial mirror. An ordinary mirror reflects what is in front of it, whereas the living mirror we carry within us reflects in quite another way. It reflects in the course of time the sense impressions we receive, causing one or another impression to be reflected back again into consciousness, and so we have a memory of a past experience.

If we break a spatial mirror, we see behind the mirror; we see into a realm we do not see when the mirror is intact. Correspondingly, if we carry out inner exercises of the soul, we come, as I have often suggested, to something like a breaking of the inner mirror. The memories can, as it were, cease for a brief time—for how long a time depends upon our free will—and we can see more deeply into our inner being. As we look more deeply into our inner being behind the memory-mirror, then what I characterized yesterday as a kind of source of destruction meets our gaze.

There must be such a source of destruction within us, for only in such a source can the I of man solidify itself. It is actually a source for the solidification and hardening of the I. As I said yesterday, if this hardening of the I, if this egoity, is carried out into social life, evil arises, evil in the life and actions of human beings.

You may see from this how truly complicated is the life into which man is placed. What within the human being has a good purpose, without which we could not cultivate our I, must never be allowed outside. The evil man carries it into the outer world; the good man keeps it inside him. If it is carried outside, it becomes wrong, it becomes evil. If it is kept within, it is the very thing we need to give the human I its rightful strength.

There is really nothing in the world that would not, in its place, have a beneficial significance. We would be thoughtless and rash if we did not have this source within us, for this source manifests itself in such a way that we can experience in it something we would never be able to experience in the outer world. In the outer world we see things materially. Everything we see, we see materially, and following the custom of present-day science we speak of the conservation of matter, the indestructibility of actual matter. In this source of destruction about which I spoke yesterday matter is truly annihilated. Matter is thrown back into its nothingness, and then we can allow, within this nothingness, the good to arise. The good can arise if, instead of our instincts and impulses, which are bound to work toward the cultivation of egoity, we pour into this source of destruction, by means of a moral inclination of soul, all moral and ethical ideals. Then something new arises. Then in this very source of destruction the seeds of future worlds arise. Then we, as human beings, take part in the coming into being of worlds.

When we speak, as one can find in my *Outline of Occult Science*, of how our earth will one day face annihilation, and of how through all kinds of intermediate states of transformation the Jupiter existence will evolve, we must say the following. In the Jupiter existence there will be only the new creation that already is being formed today in the human being out of moral ideals, within this source of destruction. It is also formed out of his anti-moral impulses, out of what works as evil from his egoity. Hence the Jupiter existence will be a struggle between what man on earth is already bringing to birth by carrying his moral ideals into his inner chaos and what arises with the cultivation of egoity as the anti-moral. When we look into our deepest selves, therefore, we are gazing upon a region where matter is thrown back into its nothingness.

I went on to indicate how matters stand with the other side of human existence, with the side where sense phenomena are spread out around us. We behold these sense phenomena spread around us like a tapestry, and we apply our intellect to combine and relate them in order to discover within these sense phenomena laws that we then call the laws of nature. With ordinary consciousness, however, we never penetrate through this tapestry of the senses. With ordinary consciousness we penetrate the tapestry of sense impressions just as little as we penetrate with ordinary consciousness the memory-mirror within. With a developed consciousness, however, one does penetrate it, and the human beings of ancient Oriental wisdom penetrated it with a consciousness informed by instinctive vision. They beheld that world in which egoity cannot hold its own in consciousness.

We enter this world every time we go to sleep. There the egoity is dimmed, because beyond the tapestry of the senses lies the world where, to begin with, the I-power, as it develops for human existence, has no place at all. Hence the world conception of the ancient Oriental, who developed a peculiar longing to live behind the sense phenomena, used to speak of Nirvana, of the dispersing of the egoity.

Yesterday we drew attention to the great contrast between East and West. At one time the Oriental cultivated all that man longs to behold behind the sense phenomena, and he cultivated the vision into a spiritual world that is composed not of atoms and molecules but of spiritual beings. This world was present for the ancient Oriental world conception as visible reality. In our day the Oriental, particularly in Asia but also in other parts of the world, is living in the decadent stages of development of this inner yearning to reach the world behind the sense phenomena, while the human being of the West has cultivated his egoity, has cultivated all that we have characterized as the hardening and strengthening taking place within the source of destruction in man's inner being.

In saying this we are already on the way to suggesting what it is that must necessarily be absorbed into man's consciousness, now and in the near future. If the pure intellectualism that has been developing since the middle of the fifteenth century were to continue, humanity would fall entirely into decline, for with the help of intellectualism one will never penetrate beyond either the memory-mirror or the tapestry of the world of the senses spread out before us. Man must, however, acquire once more a consciousness of these worlds. He must acquire a consciousness of these worlds if Christianity is again to be able to become a truth for him, for Christianity actually is not a truth for him today. We can see this most clearly when we look at the modern development of the idea of Christ—if indeed modern times may be said to have any such development at all. The truth is that for modern man in the present stage of evolution it is impossible to arrive at an idea of Christ as long as he makes use only of the concepts and ideas that he has been cultivating as natural science since the fifteenth century. In the nineteenth and beginning of the twentieth centuries he has become incapable of forming a true idea of Christ.

These things must be regarded in the following way. The human being beholds the world all around and uses the combining faculty of his intellect, which he now has as his modern consciousness, to build up natural laws. Following a line of thought that is perfectly possible for the consciousness of the present day, he comes to the point at which it is possible for him to say, "This world is permeated with thought, for the laws of nature are apprehended in thoughts and are actually themselves the thoughts of the world." If one follows the laws of nature to the stage at which one is bound to apply them to the coming into existence of man himself as physical being, one has to say, "Within that world which we survey with our ordinary consciousness, beginning with sense perception and going on as far as the memory-mirror, a spiritual element is living." One must actually be ill, pathological, if, like the ordinary atheistic materialist, one is not willing to acknowledge this spiritual element. We live within this world that is given for ordinary consciousness; we emerge into it as physical man through physical conception and physical birth. What is observable within the physical world can only be contemplated inadequately if one fails to see as its foundation a universal spiritual element.

We are born as physical beings from physical stock. When we are born as little babies, we are actually, for outer, physical perception, quite similar to a creature of nature. Out of such a creature of nature, which is basically in a kind of sleeping condition, inner spiritual faculties gradually develop. These inner spiritual faculties will arise in the course of future evolution. If we learn to trace back these emerging spiritual faculties in the same way that we trace the gradual growth of the limbs, we find that we must look for their source beyond birth and conception. Then one comes to the point of thinking in a living and spiritual way about the world, whereas before, in one's consideration of outer nature, one built up only abstract laws. One comes, in other words, to an affirmation of what may be called the Father God.

It is very significant that scholasticism in the Middle Ages maintained that knowledge obtainable by ordinary observation of the world through ordinary human reason included knowledge of the Father God. One can even say, as I have often expressed it, that if anyone sets out to analyze this world as it is given for ordinary consciousness and does not arrive at gathering up all the natural laws in what is called the Father God, he must actually be ill, pathological in some way. To be an atheist means to be ill, as I have said here once before.

With this ordinary consciousness, however, one cannot go farther than this Father God. This far one can go with ordinary consciousness, but no further. It is characteristic of our times when such a significant theologian as Adolf von Harnack[5] says that Christ the Son does not really belong in the Gospels, that the Gospels are the message of the Father, and that Christ Jesus actually has a place in the Gospels only insofar as He brought the message of the Father God. Here you may see quite clearly how with a certain inevitability this modern thinking leads people to recognize, even in theology, only the Father God and to understand the Gospels themselves as containing no more than the message of the Father God. In the sense of this theology, Christ has worth only insofar as He appeared in the world and brought to human beings the true teaching concerning the Father God.

Two things are implied in this. First, the belief that the message of the Father God cannot be found by an ordinary study of the world. The Scholastics still maintained that it could. They did not imagine that the Gospels were to speak of the Father God; they assumed that the Gospels were to speak of God the Son. That people can come forward with the opinion that the Gospels actually speak only of the Father God is proof that theology, too, has fallen into that way of thinking which has been cultivated as the peculiarly Western method.

In early Christian times until about the third or fourth

century A.D., when there was still a good deal of Oriental wisdom in Christianity, human beings occupied themselves intently with the question of the distinction between the Father God and God the Son. One could say that these fine distinctions between the Father God and the Son God, which so engaged people's attention in the early Christian centuries, under the influence of Oriental wisdom, have long ceased to have meaning for modern man, who has been occupied in cultivating egoity under the influences I described yesterday.

A certain untruth has thus found its way into modern religious consciousness. What man experiences inwardly, through which he arrives at his analysis and synthesis of the world, is the Father God. From tradition, he has God the Son. The Gospels speak of Him, tradition speaks of Him. Man has the Christ; he wants to acknowledge Him but through inner experience no longer actually has the Christ. He therefore takes what he *should* apply actually only to the Father God and transfers it to the Christ God. Modern theology does not actually have the Christ at all; it has only the Father, but it calls the Father "Christ," because at one time it received the tradition of the Christ being in history, and one wants to be Christian, of course. If one were honest, one would be unable to call oneself a Christian in modern times.

All this is altogether different when we go further East. Already in Eastern Europe it is different. Take the Russian philosopher of whom I have frequently spoken—Soloviev.[6] You find in him an attitude of soul that has become a philosophy and speaks with full justification, with an inner justification, of a distinction between the Father and the Son. Soloviev is justified in speaking in this way, because for him both the Father and the Christ are experiences. The human being of the West makes no distinction between God the Father and Christ. If you are inwardly honest with yourselves, you will feel that the moment you wish to make a distinction between the Father God and Christ the two become confused. For Soloviev such a thing is impossible. Soloviev experiences each separately, and so he still has a sense for the battles, the spiritual battles, that were fought during the first Christian centuries in order to bring to human consciousness the distinction between the Father God and God the Son.

This, however, is the very thing to which modern man must come again. There must again be truth in calling ourselves Christians. One must not make a pretense of worshipping the Christ, attributing to Him only the qualities of the Father God. To avoid this, however, one must present truths such as I indicated yesterday. That is the only way we can come to the twofold experience, the experience of the Father and the experience of the Son.

It will be necessary to change the whole form of our consciousness. The abstract form of consciousness with which modern man is raised, and which actually does not permit the recognition of more than the Father God, will have to be replaced by a much more concrete life of consciousness. Needless to say, one cannot present such things before the world at large today in the way I have described them to you here, for people have not yet been prepared sufficiently by spiritual science and anthroposophy. There is always the possibility, however, of pointing out even to modern man how he carries in his inner being a source of destruction and how in the outer world there is something in which the I of man is, as it were, submerged, where it cannot hold itself fast—just as in earlier times people were told about the Fall of Man and similar things. One must only find the right form for these things, a form that would enable them to find their way into ordinary consciousness—even as the teaching of the Fall of Man used to give instruction concerning a spiritual foundation of the world, a form that would have a different authority from our teaching concerning the Father God.

Our modern science will have to become permeated with ways of looking such as those we have expounded here. Our science wishes to recognize in the inner being of man only the laws of nature. In this source of destruction, however, of which I have often spoken here, the laws of nature are united with the moral laws; there, natural law and moral law are one. Within our inner being matter, and with it all the laws of nature, is annihilated. Material life, together with all the laws of nature, is thrown back into chaos, and out of the chaos a new nature is able to arise, saturated with the moral impulses we ourselves lay into it. As we have said, this source of destruction is below our memory-mirror. If we let our gaze penetrate far below this memory-mirror, there at last we observe what actually is always within the human being. A human being is not changed by knowledge: he merely comes to know what he is like, what his normal condition is. Man must learn to reflect on what he is and how he lives.

When we are able to penetrate into this inner core of evil in the human being and are able also to become conscious of how into this inner evil, where matter is destroyed and thrown back into its chaos, moral impulses can find their way, then we have really found in ourselves the beginning of spiritual existence. Then we perceive the creating spirit within us, for when we behold moral laws working upon matter that has been thrown back into chaos, we are beholding a real activity of the spirit taking place within us in a natural way. We become conscious of the concrete, spiritual activity that is within us and that is the seed for future worlds.

What can we compare with what is announced in our inner being? We cannot compare it with what our senses at first convey to us of outer nature. We can compare it only with what another human being communicates when he speaks to us. Indeed, it is more than a metaphor when we say that what takes place in our inner being *speaks* to us when moral and anti-moral impulses unite themselves with the chaos inside us. There actually is within us something that speaks to us. There we have something that is not mere allegory or symbol but actual fact. What we can hear outwardly with our ears is a language toned down for the earthly world, but within our inner being a language is spoken that goes out beyond the earth, because it speaks out of what contains the seeds of future worlds. There we truly penetrate into what must be called "the inner word." In the weakened words that we speak or hear in conversation with our fellow men, hearing and speaking are separate and distinct, whereas in our inner being, when we dive down below the memory-mirror into the inner chaos, we have a substantiality where speaking becomes at the same time hearing. Hearing and speaking are once more united. The inner word speaks in us, the inner word is heard in us.

We have at the same time entered a realm where it no longer makes sense to speak of subjective and objective. When you hear another human being, when he speaks words to you that you perceive with your sense of hearing, you know that this being of another person is outside you, but you must give yourself up, must surrender yourself, as it were, in order to perceive the being of another person in what you hear him saying. On the other hand, you know that the actual word, the audible word, is not merely something subjective but is something placed into the world. Hence we find that even with the toned-down words that we hear and speak in our conversation with other human beings, the distinction between subjective and objective loses meaning. We stand with our subjectivity within objectivity, and objectivity works in us and with us in that we perceive. It is the same when we dive down to the inner word. It is not merely an inner word; it is at the same time something objective. It is not our inner being that speaks: our inner being is merely the stage upon which speaks *the world*.

It is similar for one who has insight to see, behind the

tapestry of the senses, a spiritual world, a world wherein spiritual beings of the higher hierarchies rule and weave. To begin with, he perceives these beings through an imagination; for his vision, however, they become permeated with inner life in that now he hears the Word, apparently sounding to him through himself but in reality from out of the world.

By means of love and devotion man therefore penetrates the tapestry of the senses and sees beyond; and the beings who reveal themselves to him when he thus offers up his own being in full devotion—these beings he comes to perceive with the help of what he recognizes in his inner being as inner word. We grow together with the outer world. The outer world begins to resound cosmically, as it were, when the inner word is awakened.

What I have been describing to you exists today in every human being, but he has no knowledge of it and therefore no awareness, no consciousness of it. He must first grow into such a knowledge, into such an awareness. When we learn to recognize the world with the ordinary consciousness that provides us with our intellectual concepts, we really come to recognize only the passing and the past. When we behold in the right way that with which our intellect provides us, we basically have a view back upon a world that is passing away. We can, however, find the Father God with the intellect, as I have said. What sort of consciousness, then, do we develop in relation to the Father God? The consciousness that the Father God lies at the foundation of a world revealing itself to our intellect in the course of passing away.

Yes, it is indeed so—since the middle of the fifteenth century man has developed through his intellect a special faculty for studying and observing what is perishing in the world. We analyze and test the world-corpse with our intellectual, scientific knowledge. And theologians such as

Adolph Harnack, who hold to the Father God alone, are really expounders of that part of the world that is perishing and that will pass away with the earth and disappear. They are backward-pointing individuals.

How is it then, finally, for a person who has entered so much into the spirit of what from childhood has been crammed into him as the modern natural scientific way of thinking? He learns that out there in the world are outer phenomena that arise and pass away but that matter persists, matter is the indestructible thing, and that if the earth comes to an end matter will never be destroyed. Certainly, he is told, a time will come when the earth will be one vast cemetery, but this cemetery will be composed of the very same atoms and molecules, or at least the same atoms, as are already there today. One thus applies all one's attention to what is perishing, and even when studying what is unfolding, one really studies only how what is perishing plays into what is unfolding.

It would never be possible for an Oriental to participate in this; we can see this even in the European Orient, in Eastern Europe, in the subdued philosophical feeling of Soloviev. He does not bring it to expression clearly—at least as clearly as it will have to be expressed in general consciousness in the future—but it is evident that Soloviev has still enough of the Oriental in him to see everywhere, within what is perishing, crumbling, dissolving into chaos, what is unfolding anew, the birth of what shall be in the future.

If we wish to see the reality, the actuality, we must envision it in the following way. All that we see with our senses, all that we also see of other human beings with our senses, will no longer exist one day; whatever makes itself known to eye, ear, and so on, will at some time in the future cease to be. Heaven and earth will pass away, for what we see of the stars by means of our senses also belongs to the things that are transient. Heaven and earth will pass away, but the inner word that is formed in the inner chaos of the human being, in the source of destruction, will live on after heaven and earth are no longer there; it will live on just as the seed of this year's plant will live on in the plant of next year. In the inner being of man are the seeds of world-futures. And if into these seeds human beings receive the Christ, then heaven and earth may pass away, but the Logos, the Christ, cannot pass away. Man bears in his inner being what will one day exist when all he sees around him will have ceased to be.

He must be able to say to himself: I look up to the Father God. The Father God lies at the foundation of the world that I can see with my senses. The world of the senses is His revelation, but it is nonetheless a perishing world, and it will drag the human being down with it if he is completely absorbed in it, if he is able to develop a consciousness only of the Father God. Man would then return to the Father God; he would be unable to evolve any further. There is also a new world unfolding, however, and it takes its beginning from man himself. When man ennobles his ethical ideals through the Christ consciousness, through the Christ impulse, when he forms his ethical ideals as they should be formed through the fact that the Christ has come to earth, then something comes to life in the chaos within him, seed is sown for the future, which is now not a perishing but an unfolding world.

One must have a strong feeling for the perishing and the unfolding worlds. One must feel how there is in nature a perpetual dying. Nature is colored, so to speak, by this death. In contrast to this, however, there is also in nature a continual unfolding, a continual coming to birth. This does not color nature in a way visible to the senses; yet if we approach nature with open hearts it is perceptible there.

We look out into nature and see the colors, all the colors of the spectrum, from the red at one end to the violet at the other, with all the shades in between. If we were now to mix these colors in a certain way—make them "color" one another—they would receive life. They would together become the so-called flesh color [*Inkarnat*], the color that emanates from man. When we look at nature, we are looking in a certain sense at the outspread colors of the rainbow, the sign and symbol of the Father God. If we look at man, however, it is the flesh color that speaks out of the inner being of man, for in man all the colors interpenetrate, thus taking on life, becoming living in their interpenetration. When we turn to a corpse, however, this power to take on life is entirely absent. There, that which is man is thrown back again into the rainbow, into the creation of the Father God. For the source of what makes the rainbow into the flesh color, making it into a living unity, man must look into his inner being.

Yesterday and today I have tried to lead you, perhaps in a complicated way, to an understanding of this inner being of man in its true significance. I have shown you how outer matter is thrown back into nothingness, into chaos, so that the spirit may become newly creative. If one looks at this new creativity, one realizes that the Father God works in matter, bringing it to its completion (see drawing, page 32, bright). Matter confronts us in the outer world in the greatest variety of ways, so that it is visible to us. Within our inner being, however, this matter is thrown back into its nothingness and then permeated with pure spiritual being, with our moral ideals or anti-moral ideas (red). There new life springs up.

The world must appear to us in its double aspect. We see first the Father God, creating what is outwardly visible; we see how what is outwardly visible comes to an end in man's inner being, where it is thrown back into chaos. We must feel intensely how this world, the world of the Father God, comes to its end; only then will we be able to reach an inner

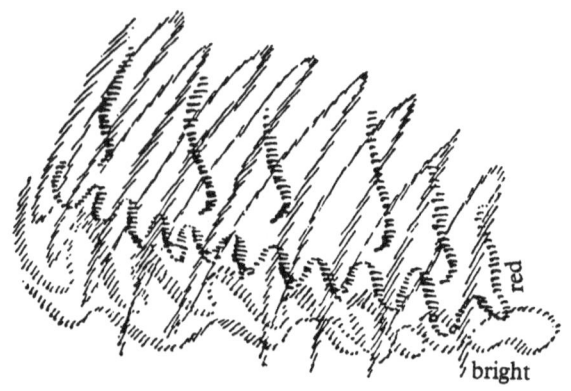

understanding of the Mystery of Golgotha. It will become clear to us through this how the very thing that comes to an end, the creation of the Father God, is endowed with life once more by God the Son; a new beginning is made.

Everywhere in the Western world it can be seen how since the fifteenth century there has been a tendency to study and investigate only the perishing, the corpse-like part of nature, which is all that is accessible to the intellect. All so-called education or culture [*Bildung*] has been formed under the influence of a science that concerns itself only with what is dead. This kind of culture is directly opposed to real Christianity. Real Christianity must have a feeling for what is living but must also be able to separate this feeling of what is reviving from what is passing away. Hence the most important idea that must be connected with the Mystery of Golgotha is the idea of the Risen Christ, the Christ Who has vanquished death. What matters is to comprehend that the most important idea is that of Christ Who passes through death and rises again. Christianity is not merely a religion of salvation; the Oriental religions were also that. Christianity is a religion of resurrection, a religion that awakens again to life what would otherwise be nothing but matter crumbling away into nothingness.

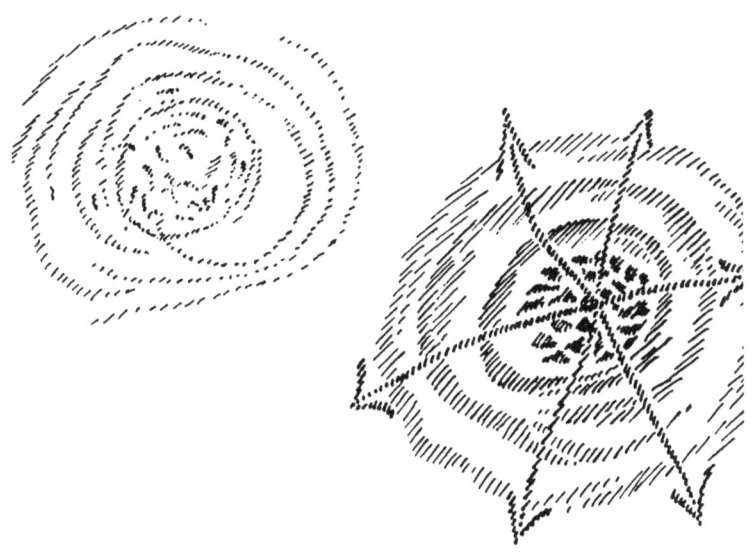

Out in the cosmos we have the crumbling away of matter in the moon, and in the sun we have a perpetual coming into being, forever new and fresh. Seen spiritually, seen through spiritual vision—when we get beyond ordinary sense perception and reach the point where Imagination is active—we can see in the moon a continuous process: it is continuously splintering and scattering itself abroad. There, where the moon is situated, its matter splinters and disperses like dust into the world. The matter of the moon is perpetually being gathered from its environment and then splintered and scattered (see drawing, above). If one looks at the moon in the consciousness of Imagination, one sees a continuous convergence of matter in the place where the moon is; it gathers there, and then it splinters and is scattered like dust into the world. The moon is actually seen like this (drawing, page 34): first a circle, then a smaller, narrower circle, becoming ever narrower until the circle becomes the moon itself. Then it dissolves, splinters; it is strewn out over the entire world. In

the moon, matter cannot tolerate a center. Matter concentrates toward the center of the moon but cannot tolerate it; it stops short there and disperses like cosmic dust. It is only to ordinary, sensory vision that the moon appears peaceful. It is not peaceful. It is continuously gathering matter together and scattering it.

When we come to the sun, we find it is all quite different. Already in Imagination we are able to see how matter does not splinter in this way at all; true, it does approach the center, but then it begins to receive life in the rays of the sun that stream out from the center. It does not splinter and disperse; it becomes living and spreads out life from the center in every direction. Together with this life it develops astrality. In the moon there is no astrality; there the astrality is destroyed. In the sun, astrality unites itself with all that streams forth. The sun is in truth something that is permeated with inner life, where the center is not only tolerated but has a fructifying influence. In the center of the sun lives the cosmic fructifying activity. In the contrast between sun and moon we thus see a cosmic manifestation of two opposite processes: in the moon matter is thrown back into chaos, while in the sun it is perpetually unfolding, springing and welling up with renewed life.

When we dive down into our inner being, we look into our inner chaos, into our own moon nature. That is the inner moon. Matter is destroyed there, as in the outer world it is destroyed only where the moon is. Then, however, the radiance of the sun penetrates our senses; the sun's radiance enters our inner moon nature. The matter inwardly dissolving there into dust is renewed by the sun's radiance. Here, in the inner being of man, matter is continuously falling under the moon influence, and just as continously man absorbs through his senses the radiance of the sun (see drawing, left). Such is the relationship in which we stand to the cosmos, and so one must have the capacity to perceive these two opposite activities in the cosmos: the moon nature directed toward splintering and scattering, and the quickening, life-giving radiance of the sun.

Through both these experiences one comes to behold, in what is splintering and crumbling to dust, the world of the Father God, which had to be there until such time as the world changed into the world of God the Son, which basically has its physical source in what is sun-like in the world. What is of the moon nature and the sun nature relate to one another as Father God to Son God.

During the early Christian centuries these things were seen instinctively. Now they must be known again with full presence of mind if the human being wishes to be able to say of himself in all honesty: I am a Christian. This is what I wished to present to you today.

III

Dornach, September 30, 1921

Today we will go somewhat further into what we considered here last Friday and Saturday, and I would like to draw your attention particularly to the life of the soul and what we discover when this soul life is viewed from the viewpoint of Imaginative cognition. You are familiar with Imaginative cognition from my book, *Knowledge of the Higher Worlds and its Attainment*. You know that we distinguish four stages of cognition, ascending from our ordinary consciousness, the stage of cognition that is adapted to our daily normal life, to ordinary modern science, and that constitutes the actual consciousness of the time. This stage of consciousness is called "objective cognition" in the sense of what is described in *Knowledge of the Higher Worlds*. Then one comes into the realm of the supersensible through the stages of Imagination, Inspiration, and Intuition. With ordinary objective cognition it is impossible to observe the soul element. What pertains to the soul must be experienced, and in experiencing it one develops objective cognition. Real cognition can be gained, however, only when one can place the thing to be known objectively before one. It is impossible to do this with the soul life in ordinary consciousness; to understand the life of the soul, one must draw back a stage, as it were, so that the life of the soul comes to stand outside one; then it can be observed. This is precisely what is brought about through Imaginative cognition, and today I would like simply to describe for you what is then brought into view.

You know that if we survey the human being, confining ourselves to what exists in the human being today, we distinguish the physical body, the etheric body or body of formative forces, which is really a sum of activities, the astral body, and the I or ego. If we now bring the soul experience not into cognition but into consciousness, we distinguish in its fluctuating life thinking, feeling, and willing. It is true that thinking, feeling, and willing play into one another in the ordinary life of the soul; you can picture no train of thought without picturing the role played in this train of thought by the will. How we combine one thought with another, how we separate a thought from another, is most definitely an act of will striving into the life of thought. Though the process may at first remain shrouded, as I have often explained, we nevertheless know that when we as human beings use our will, our thoughts play into our will as impulses. In the ordinary soul life, therefore, our will is not isolated in itself but is permeated by thought. Even more do thoughts, will impulses, and the actual feelings flow into feeling. Thus we have throughout the soul life a flowing together, yet by reason of things we cannot go into today we must distinguish, within this flowing life of soul, thinking, feeling, and willing. If you refer to my *Philosophy of Freedom*, you will see how one is obliged to loosen thinking purely from feeling and willing, because one comes to a vision of human freedom only by means of such a loosened thinking.

Inasmuch as we livingly grasp thinking, feeling, and willing we grasp at the same time the flowing, weaving life of soul. Then, when we compare what we grasp there in immediate vitality with what an anthroposophical spiritual science teaches us of the connection among the individual members of the human being—physical body, etheric body, astral body, and I—what presents itself to Imaginative cognition is the following.

We know that during waking life the physical, etheric, astral bodies, and the I are in a certain intimate connection. We know further that in the sleeping state we have a separation of the physical and etheric bodies on the one hand from the astral body and I on the other. Although it is only approximately correct to say that the I and astral body separate from the physical body and etheric body, one arrives thereby at a valid mental image. The I with the astral body is outside the physical and etheric bodies from the time we fall asleep to the moment of awakening.

As soon as the human being advances to Imaginative cognition he becomes more and more able to apprehend exactly in inner vision, with the eye of the soul, what is experienced as transitory, in *status nascendi*. The transitory is there, and one must seize it quickly, but it can be seized. One has something before one that can be observed most clearly at the moments of awaking and falling asleep. These moments of falling asleep and awaking can be observed by Imaginative cognition. Among the preparations necessary to attain higher levels of cognition you will remember that mention was made in the books already referred to of the cultivation of a certain presence of mind [*Geistesgegenwart*]. One hears so little said in ordinary life of the observations that may be made of the spiritual world, because people lack this presence of mind. Were this presence of mind actively cultivated among human beings, all people would be able to talk of spiritual, supersensible impressions, for such impressions actually crowd in upon us to the greatest extent as we fall asleep or awake, particularly as we awake. It is only because this presence of mind is cultivated so little that people do not notice these impressions. At the moment of awaking a whole world appears before the soul. As quickly as it arises, however, it fades again, and before people think to grasp it, it is gone. Hence they can speak little of this whole world that appears before the soul and that is indeed of particular significance in comprehending the inner being of man.

When one is actually able to grasp the moment of awaking with this presence of mind, what confronts the soul is a whole world of flowing thoughts. There need be nothing of fantasy; one can observe this world with the same calm and self-possession with which one observes in a chemical laboratory. Nevertheless, this flowing thought world is there and is quite distinct from mere dreams. The mere dream is filled with reminiscences of life, whereas what takes place at the moment of awaking is not concerned with reminiscences. These flowing thoughts are clearly to be distinguished from reminiscences. One can translate them into the language of ordinary consciousness, but fundamentally they are foreign thoughts, thoughts we cannot experience if we do not grasp them in the moment made possible for us by spiritual scientific training, or even in the moment of awaking.

What is it that we actually grasp at such a moment? We have penetrated into the etheric body and physical body with our I and astral body. What is experienced in the etheric body is experienced, however, as dreamlike. One learns, in observing this subtly in presence of mind, to distinguish clearly between this passing through the etheric body, when life reminiscences appear dreamlike, and the state—before fully awaking, before the impressions that the senses have after awaking—of being placed in a world that is thoroughly a world of weaving thoughts. These thoughts are not experienced, however, as dream thoughts, such as one knows are in oneself subjectively. The thoughts that I mean now confront the penetrating I and astral body of man entirely objectively; one realizes distinctly that one must pass right through the etheric body, for as long as one is passing through the etheric body, everything remains dreamlike. One must also pass through the abyss, the intermediate space—to express myself figuratively and perhaps therefore more clearly—the space between etheric body and physical body. Then one slips fully into the etheric-physical on awaking and receives the outer physical impressions of the senses. As soon as one has slipped into the physical body, the outer physical sense impressions are simply there. What we experience as a thought-weaving of an objective nature takes place completely between the etheric body and the physical body. We must therefore see in it an interplay of the etheric and physical bodies. If we present this pictorially (see drawing), we can say that if this represents the physical body (orange) and this the etheric body (green), we have the living weaving of physical body and etheric body in the thoughts that we grasp there. Through this observation one comes to know that whether we are asleep or awake processes are always taking place between our physical body and etheric body, processes that actually consist of the weaving thought-existence between our physical and etheric bodies (yellow). We have now grasped objectively the first element of the life of the soul; we see in it a weaving between the etheric body and the physical body.

This weaving life of thought does not actually come into our consciousness as it is in the waking state. It must be

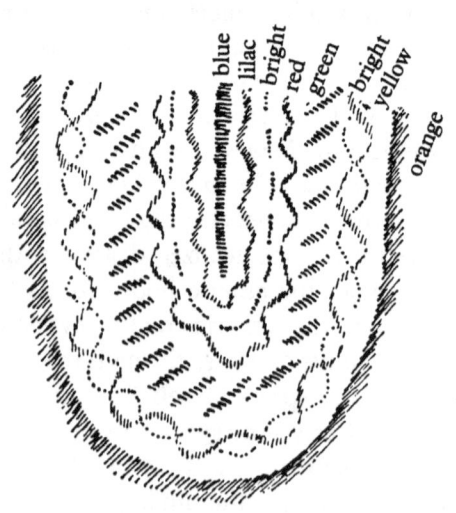

grasped in the way I have described. When we awake we slip with our I and astral body into our physical body. I and astral body within our physical body, permeated by the etheric body, take part in the life of sense perception. By having within you the life of sense perception, you become permeated with the thoughts of the outer world, which can form in you from the sense perceptions and have then the strength to drown this objective thought-weaving. In the place where otherwise the objective thoughts are weaving, we form out of the substance of this thought-weaving, as it were, our everyday thoughts, which we develop in our association with the sense world. I can say that into this objective weaving of thought there plays the subjective thought-weaving (bright) that drowns the other and that also takes place between the etheric body and the physical body. In fact, when we weave thoughts with the soul itself we live in what I have called the space between the etheric and physical bodies—as I said, this expression is figurative, but to make this understandable I must designate it as the space between the etheric and physical bodies. We drown the objective thoughts, which are always present in the sleeping and waking states, with our subjective weaving of thought. Both, however, are present in the same region, as it were, of our human nature: the objective weaving of thought and the subjective thought-weaving.

What is the significance of the objective thought-weaving? When the objective thought-weaving is perceived, when the moment of awaking is actually grasped with the presence of mind I have described, it is grasped not merely as being of the nature of thought but as what lives in us as forces of growth, as forces of life in general. These life forces are united with the thought-weaving; they permeate the etheric or life body inwardly and shape the physical body outwardly. What we perceive as objective weaving of thought when we can seize the moment of awaking with presence of mind, we perceive as thought-weaving on the one hand and as activity of growth and nutrition on the other. What is within us in this way we perceive as an inner weaving, but one that is fully living. Thinking loses its picture-nature and abstractness, it loses all that had been sharp contours. It becomes a fluctuating thinking but is clearly recognizable as thinking nevertheless. Cosmic thinking weaves in us, and we experience how this cosmic thinking weaves in us and how we plunge into this cosmic thinking with our subjective thinking. We have thus grasped the soul element in a certain realm.

When we now go further in grasping the waking moment in presence of mind we find the following. When we are able to experience the dreamlike element in passing through the etheric body with the I and astral body, we can bring to mind pictorially the dreamlike element in us. These dream pictures must cease the moment we awake, however, for otherwise we would take the dream into the ordinary, conscious waking life and be daydreamers, thus losing our self-possession. Dreams as such must cease. The usual experience of the dream is an experience of reminiscing, is actually a later memory of the dream; the ordinary experiencing of the dream is actually first grasped as a reminiscence after the dream departs. It may be grasped while it exists, however, while it actually *is*, if one carries the presence of mind right back to the experience of the dream. If it is thus grasped directly, during the actual penetration of the etheric body, then the dream is revealed as something mobile, something that one experiences as substantial, within which one feels oneself. The picture-nature ceases to be merely pictorial; one has the experience that one is within the picture. Through this feeling that one is within the picture, one is in movement with the soul element; as in waking life one's body is in movement through various movements of the legs and hand, so actually does the dream become active. It is thus experienced in the same way as one experiences the movement of an arm, leg, or head; when one experiences the grasping of the dream as something substantial, then in the further progress toward awakening yet another experience is added. One feels that the activity experienced in the dream, when one stands as if within something real, dives down into our bodily nature. Just as in thinking we feel that we penetrate to the boundary of our physical body, where the sense organs are, and perceive the sense impressions with the thinking, so we now feel that we plunge into ourselves with what we experience in the dream as inner activity. What is experienced at the moment of awaking, or rather just before the moment of awaking, when one is within the dream, still completely outside the physical body but already within the etheric body, or passing through it—is submerged into our organization. And if one is so advanced that one has this submerging as an experience, then one knows, too, what becomes of what has been submerged—it radiates back into our waking consciousness, and it radiates back as a feeling, as feeling. The feelings are dreams that have been submerged into our organization.

When we perceive what is weaving in the outer world in this dreamlike state, it is in the form of dreams. When dreams dive down into our organization and become conscious from within outward, we experience them as feelings. We thus experience feeling through the fact that what is in our astral body dives down into our etheric body and then further into our physical organization, not as far as the senses and therefore not to the periphery, but only into the inner organization. Then, when one has grasped this, has beheld it first through Imaginative cognition, particularly clearly at the moment of awaking, one also receives the inner strength to behold it continuously. We do indeed dream continuously throughout waking life. It is only that we overpower the dream with the light of our thinking consciousness, our conceptual life [*Vorstellungsleben*]. One who can gaze beneath the surface of the conceptual life—and one trains oneself for this by grasping the moment of the dream itself with presence of mind—whoever has so trained himself that on awaking he can grasp what I have described, can then also, beneath the surface of the light-filled conceptual life, experience the dreaming that continues throughout the day. This is not experienced as dreams, however, for it immediately dives down into our organization and rays back as the world of feeling. What feeling is takes place between the astral body (bright in drawing, page 40) and the etheric body. This naturally expresses itself in the physical body. The actual source of feeling, however, lies between the astral body and the etheric body (red). Just as for the thought life the physical and etheric bodies must cooperate in a living interplay, so must etheric body and astral body be in living interplay for the life of feeling. When we are awake we experience this living interplay of our mingled etheric and astral bodies as our feeling. When we are asleep we experience what takes place in the astral body, now living outside the etheric body, as the pictures of the dream. These dream pictures now are present throughout the period of sleep but are not perceptible to the ordinary consciousness; they are remembered in those fragments that form the ordinary life of dream.

You see from this that if we wish to grasp the life of the soul we must look between the members of the human organization. We think of the life of the soul as flowing thinking, feeling, and willing. We grasp it objectively, however, by looking into the spaces between these four members, between the physical body and the etheric body and between the etheric body and the astral body.

I have often explained here from other viewpoints how what is expressed in willing is withdrawn entirely from ordinary waking consciousness. This ordinary consciousness is aware of the mental images by which we direct our willing.

It is also aware of the feelings that we develop in reference to the mental images as motives for our willing and of how what lies clear in our consciousness as the conceptual content of our willing plays downward when I move an arm in obedience to my will. What actually goes on to produce the movement does not come into ordinary consciousness. As soon as the spiritual investigator makes use of Imagination and discovers the nature of thinking and feeling he can also come to a consciousness of man's experiences between falling asleep and awaking. By the exercises leading to Imagination, the I and astral body are strengthened; they become stronger in themselves and learn to experience themselves. In ordinary consciousness one does not have the true I. What do we have as the I in our ordinary consciousness? This must be explained by a comparison I have made repeatedly. You see, when one looks back upon life in the memory, it appears as a continuous stream, but it is definitely not that. We look back over the day to the moment of awaking, then we have an empty space, then the memory of the events of the previous day links itself on, and so forth. What we observe in this reminiscence bears in itself also those states that we have not lived through consciously, that are therefore not within the present content of our consciousness. They are there, however, in another form. The reminiscing of a person who never slept at all—if I may cite such a hypothetical case—would be completely destroyed. The reminiscence would in a way blind him. All that he would bring to his consciousness in reminiscence would seem quite foreign to him, dazzling and blinding him. He would be overpowered by it and would have to eliminate himself entirely. He would not be able to feel himself within himself at all. Only because of the intervals of sleep is reminiscence dimmed so that we are able to endure it. Then it becomes possible to assert our own self in our remembering. We owe it solely to the intervals of sleep that we have our self-assertion in memory. What I am now saying could well be confirmed through a comparative observation of the course of different human lives.

In the same way that we feel the inner activity in reminiscence, we actually feel our I from our entire organism. We feel it in the way we perceive the sleeping conditions as the darkest spaces in the progress of memory. We do not perceive the I directly in ordinary consciousness; we perceive it only as we perceive the sleeping condition. When we attain Imaginative cognition, however, this I really appears, and it is of the nature of will. We notice that what creates a feeling inclining us to feel sympathy or antipathy with the world, or whatever activates willing in us, then comes about in a process similar to that taking place between being awake and falling asleep. This again can be observed with presence of mind if one develops the same capacities for observation of the process of going to sleep as those I have described for awaking. Then one notices that on going to sleep one carries into the sleeping condition what streams as activity out of our feeling life, streaming into the outer world. One then learns to recognize how every time one actually brings one's will into action one dives into a state similar to the sleeping state. One dives into an inner sleep. What takes place once when one falls asleep, when the I and astral body draw themselves out of the physical body and the etheric body, goes on inwardly every time we use our will.

You must be clear, of course, that what I am now describing is far more difficult to grasp than what I described before, for the moment of going to sleep is generally still harder to grasp with presence of mind than that of awaking. After awaking we are awake and have at least the support of reminiscing. If we wish to observe the moment of falling asleep we must continue the waking state right into sleep. A person generally goes straight to sleep, however; he does not bring the activity of feeling into the sleeping state. If he can continue it, however—and this is actually possible through training—then in Imaginative cognition one notices that in willing there is in fact a diving into the same element into which we dive when we fall asleep. In willing we actually become free of our organization; we unite ourselves with real objectivity. In waking we enter our etheric and physical bodies and pass right up to the region of the senses, thus coming to the periphery of the body, taking possession of it, saturating it entirely. Similarly, in feeling we send our dreams back into the body, inasmuch as we immerse ourselves inwardly; the dreams, in fact, become feelings. If now we do not remain in the body but instead, without going to the periphery of the body, leave the body inwardly, spiritually, then we come to willing. Willing, therefore, is actually accomplished independently of the body. I know that much is implied in saying this, but I must present it, because it is a reality. In grasping it we come to see that—if we have the I here (see drawing, page 40, blue)—willing takes place between the astral body and the I (lilac).

We can therefore say that we divide the human being into physical body, etheric body or body of formative forces, astral body, and I. Between the physical body and the etheric body thinking takes place in the soul element. Between the etheric body and the astral body feeling takes place in the soul element, and between the astral body and the I, willing takes place in the soul element. When we come to the periphery of the physical body we have sense perception. Inasmuch as by way of our I we emerge out of ourselves, placing our whole organization into the outer world, willing becomes action, the other pole of sense perception (see drawing page 40).

In this way one comes to an objective grasp of what is experienced subjectively in flowing thinking, feeling, and willing. Experience metamorphoses into cognition. Any psychology that tries to grasp the flowing thinking, feeling, and willing in another way remains formal, because it does not penetrate to reality. Only Imaginative cognition can penetrate to reality in the experience of the soul.

Let us now turn our gaze to a phenomenon that has accompanied us, as it were, in our whole study. We said that through observation with presence of mind at the moment of awaking, when one has slipped through the etheric body, one can see a weaving of thoughts that is objective. One at first perceives this objective thought-weaving. I said that it can be distinguished clearly from dreams and also from the everyday life of thought, from the subjective life of thought, for it is connected with growth, with becoming. It is actually a real organization. If one grasps what is weaving there, however, what, if one penetrates it, one perceives as thought-weaving; if one inwardly feels it, touches it, I would like to say, then one is aware of it as force of growth, as force of nutrition, as the human being in the process of becoming. It seems at first something foreign, but it is a world of thought. If one can study it more accurately it is seen to be the inner weaving of thoughts in ourselves. We grasp it at the periphery of our physical body; before we arrive at sense perception we grasp it. When we learn to understand it more exactly, when we have accustomed ourselves to its foreignness compared with our subjective thinking, then we recognize it. We recognize it as what we have brought with us through our birth from earlier experiences, from experiences lying before birth or conception. For us it becomes something of the spiritual, objectively present, that brings our whole organism together. Pre-existent thought gains objectivity, becomes objectively visible. We can say with an inner grasp that we are woven out of the world of spirit through thought. The subjective thoughts that we add stand in the sphere of our freedom. Those thoughts that we behold there form us, they build up our body from the weaving of thought. They are our past karma (see diagram, page 51). Before we arrive at sense perceptions, therefore, we perceive our past karma.

When we go to sleep, one who lives in objective cognition sees something in this process of falling asleep that is akin to willing. When willing is brought to complete consciousness one notices quite clearly that one sleeps in one's own organism. Just as dreams sink down, so do the motives of the will pass into our organization. One sleeps into the organism. One learns to distinguish this sleeping into the organism, which first comes to life in our ordinary actions. These indeed are accomplished outwardly; we accomplish them between awaking and going to sleep, but not everything that lives within our life of feeling lives into these actions. We go through life also between falling asleep and awaking. What we would otherwise press into the actions, we press out of ourselves through the same process in going to sleep. We press a whole sum of will impulses out into the purely spiritual world in which we find ourselves between going to sleep and awaking. If through Imaginative cognition we learn to observe the will impulses that pass over into our spiritual being, which we shelter only between falling asleep and awaking, we perceive in them the tendency to action that exists beyond death, that passes over with us beyond death.

Willing is developed between the astral body and the I. Willing becomes deed when it goes far enough toward the outer world to come to the place to which otherwise the sense impressions come. In going to sleep, however, a large quantity goes out that would like to become deed but in fact does not become deed, remaining bound to the I and passing with it through death into the spiritual world.

You see, we experience here on the other side (see diagram, page 51) our future karma. Our future karma is experienced between willing and the deed. In Imaginative consciousness both are united, past and future karma, what weaves and lives within us, weaving on beneath the threshold above which lie the free deeds we can accomplish between birth and death. Between birth and death we live in freedom. Below this region of free willing, however, which actually has an existence only between birth and death, there weaves and lives karma. We perceive its effects out of the past if we can maintain our consciousness in our I and astral body in penetrating through the etheric body as far as to the physical body. On the other hand, we perceive our future karma if we can maintain ourselves in the region that lies between willing and the deed, if we can develop so much self-discipline through exercises that inwardly we can be as active in a feeling as, with the help of the body, we can be in a deed, if we can be active in spirit in feeling, if we therefore hold fast to the deed in the I.

Picture this vividly; one can be as enthusiastic, as inwardly enamored by something that springs from feeling as that which otherwise passes over into action; but one must withold it: then it lights up in Imagination as future karma.

What I have described to you here is of course always present in the human being. Every morning on awaking man passes the region of his past karma; every evening on falling asleep he passes that of his future karma. Through a certain attentive awareness and without special training, the human being can grasp with presence of mind the past objectivity, without, it is true, recognizing it as plainly as I have now described it. He can perceive it, however; it is there. There, too, is all that he bears within him as moral impulses of good and evil. Through this the human being actually learns to know himself better than when he becomes aware in the moment of awaking of the weaving of thought that forms him.

More difficult to grasp, however, is the perception of what lies between willing and the deed, of what one can withhold. There one learns to know oneself insofar as one has made oneself during his life. One learns to know the inner formation that one carries through death as future karma.

I wished to show you today how these things can be spoken about out of a living comprehension, how anthroposophy is not in the least exhausted in its images. Things can be described in a living way, and tomorrow I will go further in this study, going on to a still deeper grasp of the human being on the basis of what we have studied today.

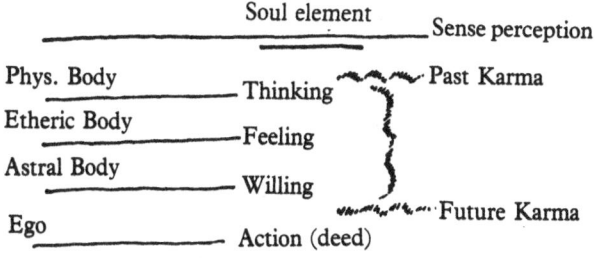

IV

Dornach, October 1, 1921

We saw yesterday how the human being in his consciousness approaches the world from two sides, as it were: when he is active from within and when he is active from without. The ordinary consciousness, however, is not able to grasp what lives within the human being, because consciousness strikes up against it. We have seen, moreover, how karma also lives in man from two sides between birth and death. On the one hand there is the moment of awaking when man plunges into his etheric body, where, while he is submerged, he can have the reminiscence of dreams in ordinary consciousness. Then he passes, as it were, the space between the etheric body and the physical body—he is in the physical body only when he has full sense perception—and there he passes through the region of the living thoughts active within him. These are the same thoughts that actually have taken part in building up his organism and that he has brought with him through birth into existence; they represent, in other words, his completed karma. On falling asleep, however, man strikes up against that which cannot become deed. What enters into deeds as our impulses of will and feeling is lived out during our lifetime. Something is always left behind, however, and this is taken by the human being into sleep. Yet it is also present at other times. Everything in the soul life that does not pass into deed, that stops short, as it were, before the deed, is future karma, which is forming itself and which we can carry further through death.

Yesterday I sought to indicate briefly how the forces of karma live in the human being. Today we will consider something of the human environment to show how the human being actually stands within the world, in order to be able to give all this a sort of conclusion tomorrow. We tried yesterday to examine objectively the human soul life itself, and we found that thinking develops itself in that region which is in fact the objective thought region between the physical body and the etheric body. We also found that feeling develops itself between the etheric and astral bodies, and willing develops itself between the astral body and the I or ego. The actual activity of the soul thus develops itself in the spaces between—I said yesterday that this expression is not exact, yet it is comprehensible—the spaces that we must suppose are between the four members of human nature, between the physical body, etheric body, astral body, and I. If we wish to view the spaces between objectively, they are the interactions among the members of the human being.

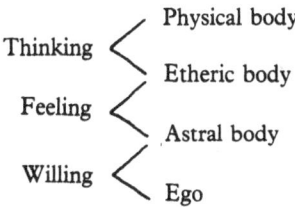

Today we wish to look at something of the human environment. Let us bring to mind clearly how the human being is in a fully living dream life, how he has pictures sweeping through the dream life. I explained yesterday that the Imaginative consciousness can perceive how these pictures descend into the organization and how what works in these pictures brings about our feelings. Our feelings are therefore what actually would be grasped if one were to look more deeply into man's inner being as an approach to dream pictures. Feelings are the waves that mount up from the day's dream life into our consciousness. We dream continuously, as I said yesterday, beneath the surface of the conceptual life, and this dream life lives itself out in feelings.

If we now look into the environment of the human being and consider first the animal world, we find in the animal world a consciousness that does not rise to thinking, to a life of thought, but that is developed actually in a sort of living dream life. We can form a picture of what reveals itself in the soul life of the animal through a study of our own dream life. The soul life of the animal is entirely a dreaming. The animal's soul life thus is much more actively at work on the organism than the soul life of man, which is more free of the organism through the clarity of the conceptual life. The animal actually dreams. Just as our dream pictures, those dream pictures that we form during waking consciousness, stream upward as feelings, so is the soul life of the animal based mainly on feeling. The animal actually does not have a soul life penetrated by the clear light of thought. What therefore takes place in us between the etheric body and the astral body is essentially what is taking place in the animal. It forms the animal's soul life, and we can understand animal life if we can picture it as proceeding from the soul life.

It is important to form a certain image of these relationships, for then one will comprehend what actually takes place when, let us say, the animal is digesting. Just watch a herd lying in a field digesting. The whole mood of the creatures reveals the truth of what has come to light through spiritual research, namely, that the aroused activity taking place essentially between the etheric body and astral body of the animal presses upward in a living feeling and that the creature lives in this feeling. The animal experience consists essentially of an enhancement and a diminishing of this feeling, and, when the feeling is somewhat subdued, of a participation in its dream pictures, the picture taking the place of feeling. We can say, therefore, that the animal lives in a consciousness that is similar to our dream consciousness.

If we seek for the consciousness that we ourselves have as human beings here on earth, we cannot look for it within the animal; we must seek it in beings who do not come to immediate physical existence. These we call the animal species-souls, souls that as such have no physical, bodily nature but that live themselves out through the animals. We can say that all lions together have such a species-soul, which has a spiritual existence. It has a consciousness such as we human beings have, not like that of the single animal.

If we now descend to the plant world we find there not the same sort of consciousness as an animal's but a consciousness similar to the one we have between sleeping and awaking. The plant is a sleeping being. We also, however, develop this consciousness between the astral body and the I in willing. What is active in the plant world is of essentially the same nature as what lives in our willing. In our willing we actually sleep even when we are awake. The same activity that prevails in our willing actually prevails over the whole plant world. The consciousness that we develop as sleep consciousness is something that actually continues as an unconscious element inserted into our conscious element, forming gaps in our memory, as I described yesterday. Our consciousness is dull during sleep, however, indeed altogether extinguished for most people, just as is the case in plant consciousness.

If we then look in plant life for what corresponds to animal life, we cannot seek it in the individual plant but must seek it in the whole earth-soul. The whole earth-soul has a dreaming consciousness and sleeps itself into the plant consciousness. Only insofar as the earth takes part in cosmic becoming does it flicker up in such a way that it can develop a full consciousness such as we human beings have in the waking state between birth and death. This is chiefly the case, however, in the time of winter, when there is a kind of waking of the earth, whereas the dull dream consciousness exists during the warm time, in summer. I have often explained in earlier lectures that it is entirely wrong to conclude that the earth awakes in summer and sleeps in winter. The reverse is true. In the stirring vegetative activity that develops during the summer, during the warm time of the year, the earth exists in a sleeping, or rather in a dreaming, state, while the waking state exists in the cold time of the year.

If we now descend to the mineral realm we must admit that the consciousness there is still deeper than that of our sleep, a consciousness that indeed lies far from our ordinary human experience, going out even beyond our willing. Nevertheless, what lives in the mineral as a state of consciousness lies far from us only apparently, only for the ordinary consciousness. In reality it does not lie far from us at all. When, for instance, we pass from willing to real action, when we perform some action, then our willing cuts itself off from us. That within which we then swim, as it were, that within which we weave and live in carrying out the deed (which, in fact, we only picture [*vorstellen*]—our consciousness does not penetrate the action, we only picture it) but what penetrates the deed itself, the content of the deed, is ultimately the same as what penetrates the other side of the surface of the mineral in mineral nature and that constitutes the mineral consciousness. If we could sink still deeper into unconsciousness we would actually come to where the mineral consciousness is weaving. We would find ourselves, however, in the same condition as that in which our action itself is also accomplished. The mineral consciousness thus lies for us on the other side of what we as human beings are able to experience. Our own deed, however, also lies on the other side of what we human beings can experience. Insofar, therefore, as our deed does not depend on us, does not lie in the sphere of what is encompassed within our freedom, our deed is just as much an event of the world as what takes place in the mineral kingdom. We incorporate our deed into this event and thus actually carry man's relation to his environment to the point where man with his action even comes over to the other side of his sleeping consciousness.

In becoming aware of the mineral world around him and seeing the minerals from the outside, the human being hits upon what lies beyond his experience. We could say that if this (see drawing) represents the circumference of what we see within the human realm, the animal realm, and the plant realm, and then we come here to the mineral realm, the mineral realm shows us only its outer side in its working upon our senses. On the other side, however, where we can no longer enter, the mineral realm develops—turned away from us, as it were—its consciousness (red). It is the consciousness that is developed there that is received from the inner contents of our deeds, that can work further in the course of our karma.

Now let us pass on to the beings who do not stand beneath the human being in the ranks of the realms of nature but who stand above the human being. How can we receive a certain mental image of these beings; how, for the con-

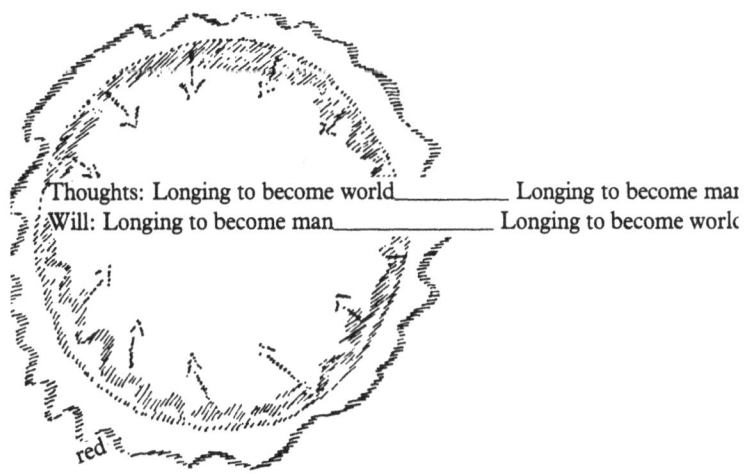

Thoughts: Longing to become world_____ Longing to become man
Will: Longing to become man_____ Longing to become worlc

sciousness that we must establish through spiritual research, through anthroposophy, can a mental image of such higher beings be formed? You know from the presentation in my book, *Knowledge of the Higher Worlds and its Attainment*, and from lectures I have given on the subject that we can ascend from the day consciousness, which we call the objective consciousness, to Imaginative consciousness. If we ascend to Imaginative consciousness in a healthy way, we first become free of our bodily nature. We weave in the ether life. Our mental images will thereby cease to have sharp contours, they will be Imaginations flowing into one another. Moreover, they will resemble the thought life that I characterized yesterday and that we find on awaking between the etheric body and the physical body. We become accustomed to such a thought life. In this thought life to which we become accustomed in Imagination, we do not link one thought to another in free will; rather, the thoughts link themselves to one another. It is a thought organism, a pictorial thought organism to which we grow accustomed. This pictorial thought organism possesses, however, the force of life. It presents itself to us as being of thought substance, but also as actually living. It has a life of its own: not the individual life possessed by physical, earthly things but a life that fundamentally lives and weaves through all things. We live into a world that lives in imagining, whose activity is imagining.

This is the world that is first experienced above the human being, this weaving world, this self-imagining world. What is woven in us between our etheric and physical bodies, which we can find on awaking and know to be identical with what enters through conception and birth into this physical world from the spiritual world, this we find only as a fragment, as something cut out of this weaving, self-imagining world. That world which is the self-imagining world finally dismisses us, and then it works still further after our birth in our physical body. There a weaving of thought takes place that is unrelated to our own subjective thought-weaving. This weaving of thought takes place in our growth. This weaving of thought is active as well in our nourishment. This weaving of thought is formed out of the universal thought-weaving of the cosmos.

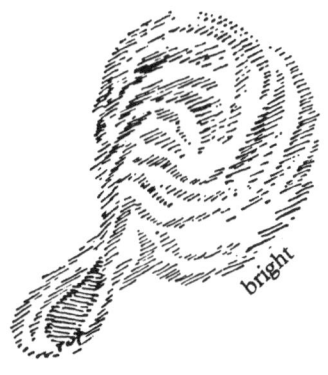

We cannot understand our etheric body without understanding that we have this universal thought-weaving of the world (see drawing, bright) and that our etheric body (red) is woven, as it were, out of this thought-weaving of the world through our birth. The thought-weaving of the world weaves into us, forms the forces that underlie our etheric body and that actually manifest themselves in the space between etheric body and physical body. They are drawn in, as it were, through the physical body, separated from the outer world, and then they work in us with the help of the etheric body, the actual body of formative forces.

We thus can picture what is behind our world. The cognition next to ours is the Imaginative, and the next state of being that is in our environment is the self-imagining one, expressing itself in living pictures. Such an expression in living pictures underlies our own organization. In our etheric body we are entirely formed and fashioned out of the cosmos. As we have to ascribe to the animal in the realm below us a consciousness like our dreaming consciousness, so in rising upward we find what we then have subjectively in Imagination. What we cultivate inwardly as a web of Imaginations exists for us outwardly; we behold it, as it were, from outside. We imagine from within. The beings just above man imagine themselves from without, revealing themselves through Imagination driven outward, and we ourselves are formed out of this world through such an Imagination driven outward. Thus in fact a weaving of thoughts, a weaving of picture-thoughts, underlies our world, and when we seek the spiritual world we find a weaving of picture-thoughts.

You know that in the development of our cognitional capacities the next stage is the stage of Inspiration. We can experience Imagination from within as a process of cognition. The next world beyond the world of self-imagining, however, is one that weaves and lives in the same element we hit upon with Inspiration, only for this world it is an "ex-spiration," a spreading out of oneself, as it were. We inspire ourselves with knowing. What the next world does, however, is to "exspire" itself; it drives outward what we drive inward in Inspired cognition.

By beholding from the reverse side what we experience inwardly as Inspiration, we thus arrive at the objectivity of the next higher beings, and so it is also with Intuition, with Intuitive cognition. I must first say, however, that if as human beings we were merely spun out of the thought-weaving of the world, we would not bring with us into this life the element of our soul that has gone through the life between the last death and this birth. What is spun out of the universal thought-weaving of the world has been assigned to us by the cosmos. Now, however, the soul element must enter it. The entry of the soul element is through such an activity of "exspiration," through an activity that is the reverse of Inspiration. We are thus "exspired" from the soul-spiritual world. Inasmuch as the cosmos weaves around us with its thought-weaving, the soul-spiritual world permeates us in "exspiring" with the soul element. First, however, it must receive this soul element, and here we come to something that can be comprehended correctly only through the human being.

You see, as human beings living in the world between birth and death we continuously receive impressions of the outer world through our sense perceptions. We form mental images about these and permeate our mental images with our feelings. We pass over to our will impulses and permeate all these. This forms in us at first, however, a kind of abstract life, a kind of picture life. If you look from within, as it were, at what the sense organs have formed inwardly as soul experience of the outer world, you find, in fact, the content of your soul. It is the soul content of the human being that in the higher waking consciousness presents what the outer world gives him between birth and death. His inner being receives it, as it were. If I sketch this inner being, in perception the world as it were enters (see drawing, page 62, *red*), becomes inwardly penetrated by the forces of feeling and will, and presses itself into the human organism. We actually bear within us a view of the world, but we bear this view of the world through the effects, the impressions, of the world pressing into us. We are not able to understand fully in our ordinary consciousness the destiny of what actually goes on in us with these impressions of the world. What presses into us and—within certain limits—what is a picture of the cosmos is not only permeated by feelings and inner will impulses, which enter us in consciousness, but is pulsed through by all that otherwise lives within the human being. In this way it acquires a certain tendency. For as long as we live, right up until death, it is held together by the body. In penetrating the portal of death, it takes with it from the body what one can call a wish to continue what it became in the body, a wish to accept the being of man. When we carry our inner soul life through death it acquires the wish to accept the being of man.

That is what our soul life bears through death: the longing for the being of man. And this longing for the being of man is particularly strongly expressed in all that is dreaming and sleeping in the depths of our soul life, in our will. Our will, as it incorporates itself into the soul life, which arises out of the impressions of the outer world, bears within it as it goes through death into a spiritual world, into the weavings of a spiritual world, the deepest longing to become man.

Our thought world, on the other hand, that world which can be seen in our memories, for example, which is reflected from us ourselves into our consciousness, bears within it the opposite longing. It has indeed formed a relationship with our human nature. Our thoughts have a strong relationship to our human nature. They then bear in themselves, when they go through death, the most intense longing to spread out into the world—to become world (see drawing, page 57).

We therefore can say that as human beings going through death our thoughts bear within them the longing to become world. The will, on the other hand, which we have developed in life, bears within it the longing to become man.

> Thoughts: Longing to become world.
> Will: Longing to be come man.

This is what goes with us through death. All that rules as will in the depths of our being bears in its deepest inner being the longings to become man. One can perceive this with Imaginative consciousness if one observes the sleeping human being, whose will is outside him, whose will with the I is outside him. In what is to be found outside the human body, the longing is already clearly expressed to return, to awake again, in order to take human shape within the extension of the human physical body itself. This longing, however, remains beyond death. Whatever is of a will nature desires to become man, whereas whatever is of a thought nature and must unite with the thoughts that are so near to the physical life, with the thoughts that actually form our human tissue and bear our human configuration between birth and death—that acquires the longing to be dispersed again, to disintegrate, to become world. This lasts until approximately the middle of the time that we spend between death and a new birth.

The thought element in its longing to become world then has come, as it were, to an end. It has incorporated itself into the entire cosmos. The longing to become world is achieved, and a reversal comes about. Midway between death and a new birth this longing of the thoughts to become world slowly changes into the longing to become man again, again to interweave itself so as to become the thought-web that we can perceive next to the body when we awake. We can say, therefore, that in the moment that lies midway between death and a new birth—which I called the Midnight Hour of Existence in my Mystery Dramas—we have a rhythmic reversal from the longing of our thoughts to become world, now that it has been fulfilled, into the longing to become man again, gradually to descend in order to become man again.

In the same moment that the thoughts receive the longing to become man again, the reverse appears in the will. The will at first develops the longing to become man in the spiritual element where we live between death and a new birth. It is this longing that predominantly fills the will. Out there between death and a new birth the will has experienced a spiritual image of the human being; now there arises in it the most vivid longing again to become world. The will spreads out, as it were; it becomes world, it becomes cosmos. By reason of this spreading out it extends even to the vicinity of the stream of nature that is formed through the line of heredity in the succession of generations. What works as will in the spiritual-physical cosmos and begins in the Midnight Hour of Existence to have the longing again to become world already lives in the flow of generations. When we then embody ourselves in the other stream that has the longing to become man, the will has preceded us in becoming world. It lives already in the propagation of the generations into which we then descend. In what we receive from our ancestors the will already lives, the will that wished to become world after the Midnight Hour of Existence. Through what in our thoughts has desired since the Midnight Hour of Existence to become man, we meet with this will-desiring-to-become-world, which then incorporates itself into what we receive from our ancestors.

Thoughts:	Longing to become world—longing to become man.
Will:	Longing to become man—longing to become world.

You see, therefore, that when we thus follow with spiritual vision what lives on the one hand in the physical and what lives on the other hand in the spiritual, we really picture man's becoming. Since we incline downward to our physical existence through the thought-web that longs to become man, however, we are there related to all the beings who live in the sphere just above man, beings who imagine themselves. We pass through the sphere of the beings who, as it were, imagine themselves. At the very moment when this reversal takes place, our soul, permeated with the I, also finds the possibility of living on in the two streams. They diverge, it is true, but the soul lives with them, cosmically lives, until, when the longing to become man again has been fully realized, it incarnates and becomes indeed an individual human being. The life of the soul is very complex, and here in the Midnight Hour of Existence it passes over the abyss. It is inspired, breathed in, out of our own past, that past at first lying between our last death and the Midnight Hour of Existence. We pass this Midnight Hour of Existence through an activity that resembles, experienced inwardly, an inspiring, and that outwardly is an "exspiration," proceeding from the former existence. When the soul has passed the Midnight Hour of Existence we come together with those beings who stand at the second stage above man and who live, as I have said, in "exspiration."

The third stage in higher cognition is Intuitive cognition. If we experience it from within, we have experienced it from one side; if we experience it from without then we have an intuiting, a self-surrender, a true surrender of self. This self-surrender, this flowing forth into the outer world, is the nature of the hierarchy that stands at the third stage above man, the "intuiting." This intuiting is the activity through which the content of our former earthly life is surrendered to our present one, streams over, pours itself into our present life on earth. We exercise this activity continually, both on the way to the Midnight Hour of Existence and beyond it. This activity permeates all else, and through it, in going through repeated earthly lives, we participate in that world in which are the beings living in real Intuition, the self-surrendering beings. We, too, out of our former earthly life, surrender ourselves to the earthly existence that follows.

We can thus gain a picture of the course of our life between death and a new birth in the environment of these three worlds. Just as here between birth and death we live in the environment of the animal, plant, and mineral worlds, so between death and rebirth we live in that world where what we otherwise grasp in Imagination lives in pictures formed from without. Hence what we carry out of the spiritual cosmos into our bodily form we can also grasp through Imagination. Our soul element, which we carry through the Midnight Hour of Existence, which lives in us principally as the activity of feeling, though dulled into the dreamlike, we can grasp through Inspired cognition, and this is also, when it appears as our life of feeling, permeated by such beings.

In fact, we live fully as human beings only in our outer sense perception. As soon as we advance to thinking, something is objective for this thinking, which is given for Imagination in picture form. We raise into our consciousness only the abstract thoughts out of the picture-forming. Immediately behind our consciousness there lies the picture-weaving of thoughts. As human beings between birth and death, we come to freedom through the fact that we can raise the abstract thoughts out of this picture-weaving. The world of Imaginative necessity lies behind, and there we are no longer alone in the same way as we are here. There we are interwoven with beings revealing themselves through Imagination, as we are then in our feeling nature interwoven with beings revealing themselves through "exspiration," through inspiring turned outward. In going from earthly life to earthly life we are interwoven with those beings who live by Intuition.

Our human life thus reaches downward into the three realms of nature and reaches upward into the three realms of the divine, soul-spiritual existence. This shows us that in our view of the human being here we have only man's outer side. The moment we look at his inner being he continues toward the higher worlds, he betrays to us, reveals to us his relationship to the higher worlds. We live into these worlds through Imagination, Inspiration, and Intuition.

With this we have gained some insight into the human environment. At the same time, however, we have discovered the world that stands as a world of spiritual necessities behind the world of physical necessities. We learn then to appreciate all the more what lies in the center: the world of our ordinary consciousness, through which we pass in the waking condition between birth and death. There we incorporate into our actual human nature what can live in freedom. Below us and above us there is no freedom. We bear freedom through the portal of death by taking with us the most essential content of the consciousness that we possess between birth and death. Indeed, the human being owes to earthly existence the mastery over what in him is the life of freedom. Then, at all events, it can no longer be taken from him, if he has mastered it by passing through life between birth and death. It can no longer be taken from him if he carries this life into the world of spiritual necessities. This earthly life receives its deep meaning precisely by our being able to insert it between what lies below us and above us. We thus rise to a grasp of what can be understood as the spiritual in the human being.

If we wish to know about the soul element, we must look into the spaces between physical body, etheric body, astral body, and I; we must look into what is weaving there between the members of our being. If we wish to acquaint ourselves with man as a spiritual being, we must ask what man experiences with the beings who imagine themselves, with the beings who reveal themselves outwardly through Inspiration, or actually through "exspiration," with the beings who reveal themselves through Intuition. If we therefore wish to examine the life of the soul we must look for the interaction developed among our human members, and if we wish to study man as a spiritual being we must look for the intercourse with the beings of the hierarchies.

When we look down into nature and wish to view the human being in his entirety, then this human being unveils itself to spiritual vision the moment we can say from inner knowledge: the human being, as he is today, bears in himself physical body, etheric body, astral body, and I. One thus has learned to recognize what man is within nature. Now we become aware—at first in a subjective way through inner experience—of the weaving of the soul. We do not behold it, we stand within it. In rising to a view of the soul we must search between the members that we have discovered as the members of man's being in natural existence. What these members do with one another from within unveils itself for us as the objective view of the soul's life.

Then, however, we must go further and must now not only seek the members of man and the effect of these members upon one another, but we must take the whole human being and see him in interaction with what lives in the widest circumference of the perceptible world environment, below him and above him. Then we discover what lives beneath him, as though sleeping in relation to what is above him, and what proves itself to be the actual spirituality of the human being—spirituality as experience of our activity with the beings of the higher hierarchies. What is experienced above as the actual spirituality and what is experienced below in nature is experienced as an alternation, a rhythmic alternation between waking and sleeping. If we go from the human consciousness, which is the waking consciousness, down to the animal consciousness, which is the dreaming consciousness, down to the plant realm, the sleeping consciousness, and if we go still deeper, we find what is deeper than sleep; if we go upward we first find Imagination as reality fulfilled. Therefore there is a further awakening in relation to our ordinary consciousness, a still further awakening with the higher beings through Inspiration and a fully awakened condition in Intuition, a condition of such awakeness that it is a surrendering to the world.

Now I beg you to follow this diagram, which is of the greatest significance for understanding the world and man. Take this as the central point, as it were, of ordinary human consciousness. It first descends and finds the animal's dreaming consciousness; it descends further and finds the plant's sleeping consciousness; it descends further and finds the mineral's deeply sleeping consciousness.

Now, however, the human being rises above himself and finds the beings who reveal themselves in Imaginations; he goes further upward and finds the beings who reveal themselves in Inspirations, actually through an "exspirating"

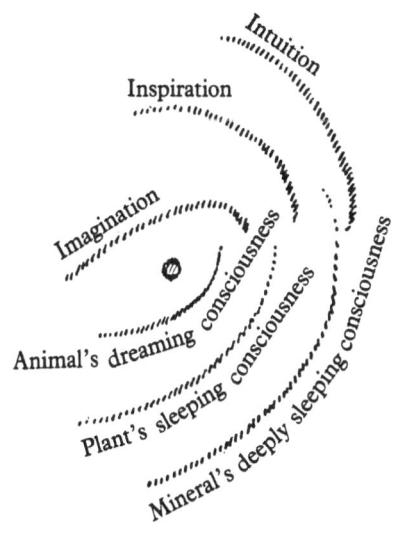

being; he finally finds the beings who reveal themselves through Intuition, who pour themselves out.

Where do they pour themselves? The highest consciousness pours itself into the deeply sleeping consciousness of the mineral realm. The mineral realm spread around us reveals one side to us. If you approached this one side and were really able to penetrate it—though not by splintering it into atoms—on the other side you would find, raying in from the opposite direction, that which, in Intuitive consciousness, streams into the deeply sleeping consciousness of the mineral realm. This process that we can find there in space we, as human beings, go through in *time* in our evolution through different earthly lives.

We will speak further about these relationships tomorrow.

V

Dornach, October 2, 1921

I would like, in order to be aware of the connections, to recapitulate briefly what we have been studying during recent days in relation to cognition of the soul-spiritual life of the human being. In particular I would like to refer to the most important things in what has been said as a sort of prelude to what has still to be added as a temporary conclusion to these studies. Today I shall speak more of the results; I have already explained the process of observation in the past few days.

We have seen that in the space between the etheric body and the physical body there exists a sort of web of living thoughts. What exactly is this web of living thoughts? It is what we bring through birth into the earthly world from the soul spiritual world. It is necessary for one to imagine that what we possess within our thinking activity merely in pictures, what therefore only reflects something within our thinking activity, has an independent life of its own. What we feel in having thoughts, however, is not within this, but the web of thought is permeated by objective being, that is to say, it is a working, weaving, active web of thought. Indeed, it works on the human being during his whole life between birth and death, helping to shape him.

I beg you to keep what I just said fully in mind. One cannot say, for instance, that the human being is formed entirely by this web of thought, that man is thus woven entirely out of what one can call world thoughts. That is not the case, at least not regarding this web of thought to be found between the etheric and physical bodies. Man is definitely constituted by something else as well, which approaches him out of the universal cosmos, and what I have described as this web of thought is only weaving with it. We find it, as it were, in the place where our subjective thinking also lies, for we weave the subjective thoughts into this web of thought. The objective thoughts do not appear to the ordinary consciousness at all, but because the subjective thoughts, which are kindled through the outer world, have their life in this web, that which is the content of our thoughts comes to our consciousness.

This, then, is the human being from the one side. It is the human being from the side of the skin, insofar as the sum of the senses is basically embodied in the skin. As soon as we approach the sense world itself today, however, the fact is that we do not come right to the senses, in looking upon them as being what was incorporated into man when he entered existence through birth. We would have to draw it like this. If this is the web of thought between the etheric body and the physical body (see drawing, right, bright), it is surrounded from outside by the sense life incorporated in the skin (red). This sense life is thus formed out of the cosmos, as it were, and incorporated into the human being. It is what man has received as a gift, as it were, from the cosmos when coming in through birth he brings what at first is in his web of thoughts. Actually, when one speaks of the human being as evolving through the Saturn, Sun, Moon, and Earth evolutions, as I have described in my *Outline of Occult Science*, one at first finds this outer evolution, begun on Saturn, expressed mainly in the configuration of the sense organs. This is continued through processes from within into the glandular system, nervous system, and so on; what the human being receives as his organization out of the cosmos, however, proceeds from the senses.

What I have drawn here as a web of thought is something that belongs fully to the individual human being. It is incor-

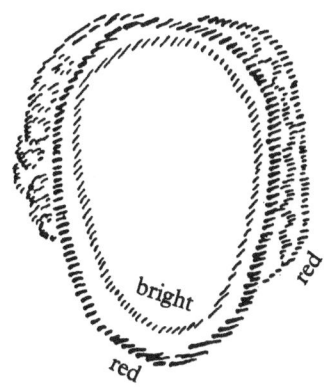

porated from the etheric world when the human being enters existence through birth, yet it definitely belongs to the individual human being, that is, it has to do with the individual earthly evolution of the human being. One can thus say that this objective thought organization works upon us during our embryonic life and during our whole life from birth to death, but it is in no way *all* that produces the entire being of man.

On the other hand we have found what is of the nature of will, and we could say that this will nature develops between the astral body and the I. The I as possessed by the human being is entirely of a will nature. During the life between birth and death the I develops, as I have indicated, in such a way that the impulses of willing pass over into deeds of the human being, though not completely; certain things remain behind. What remains behind of a will nature passes over into future karma. When we therefore consider the human begin from the point of view of his physical body, we come in the web of thought to his past karma. Looking at man from the viewpoint of the I, we must be fully conscious that it is the I that actually lives fully in his deeds, actually only first awakes in the deeds of man. What the I withholds in itself is then carried through the portal of death and passes over into future karma, the karma that is coming into existence.

Viewed objectively, therefore, we find what is otherwise in us subjectively as soul life. We find it objectified. We find that we are able to consider it objectively. We find, however, when we look toward the relationship with the subjective, that on the one side we have the thought structure and on the other we have the will structure. In the middle, for subjective experience, stands feeling.

One can arrive at the actual essence of feeling only when one is clear that actually every separate feeling that man can shelter is woven into the whole life of feeling of the human being. The feeling life of man can really be studied only when we understand it in such a way that we say: in any moment of life we are permeated by the totality of our life of feeling. We could also say that we are in a certain mood of feeling [*Gefühlstimmung*]; in every moment of our life we are in a certain mood of feeling. We should try sometime—each one, of course, can only do it individually—to bring this mood to consciousness. Let us try to bring to consciousness how in some moment of his earthly life man is in a certain mood, a certain state of feeling. You know, of course, how mood has infinite variations. It is such that it can degenerate in one case into a sort of excess gaity; one person may be gay to excess, another suffers from depression, and a third is more equable. If we merely wish to examine this mood in some moment of life, there is no need to go into its ultimate cause; we need only look at the particular shading, the particular nuance of this mood, how in one person it can approach the deepest depression, in another it can be equanimity, in a third it can reach extreme gaiety, and how thousands of intermediate stages can lie between. This mood of feeling is actually different in every human being. Now, if one explores this mood in oneself through a kind of self-knowledge, one actually finds in this mood nothing other than subjective experience, shaded in all sorts of ways by outer events, but nevertheless subjective experience.

If one remains in this subjective experience, that is, in the actual inner weaving of soul, and does not advance to beholding these things objectively, one cannot clarify to oneself the nature, let us say, of this emotional mood of soul at some given moment. One can arrive already in ordinary life, however, at what this mood is, this mood living utterly and entirely in feeling. To do so one must have above all the ability to make psychological observations. One must have the possibility of investigating particularly outstanding personalities regarding the content of their feeling. Then one can have the following experience. Outer observation, it is true, will give only an approximation of the actual truth, but even this approximation is extraordinarily valuable.

We can, for instance, set ourselves the task of studying Goethe, whom one can follow very well from his diaries, his letters, and that which has flowed into his most characteristic works. Following his biography sometimes from day to day, sometimes from morning to afternoon, we can see in his case just what were the moods of his soul [*Gemütsstimmung*]. One can, for example, set oneself the task of studying in delicate psychological ways the mood of soul that Goethe had at some particular time, let us say in 1790. One will first try to describe it as precisely as possible. One can do this, one can describe this mood as precisely as possible, but then one is pointed in two different directions—it is extraordinarily important to bear this in mind—one is pointed in two directions: to Goethe's life before 1790 and to what he lived through after 1790. When from a psychological viewpoint one compares all that impressed Goethe's soul before 1790 with what then worked upon his soul up to his death—that is, when one brings into the present the preceding and the following part of life—then the wonderful fact emerges that every momentary mood in man represents a cooperation between what has gone before, what he knows and already has consciously encountered in life, and what is yet to come and is not yet given to his conscious experience. What is still unknown to him lives already, however, in the general mood of feeling. One thus can arrive biographically, I would like to say, at this secret of the mood of soul at any moment. Here one touches the borders of those realms of human observation that are gladly neglected by people who spend their lives without much thought. What the future brings to the human being, he still does not know—or so he imagines. In his life of feeling, however, he knows it.

One can go further and make more investigations, investigating for instance, the mood of soul of some person whom one has known very well and who died, let us say, a few years after one had grasped this mood of soul. Then one can see clearly how the approaching death and all connected with it had already thrown its light back on the mood of soul. If one goes into these things, therefore, one can really see the person's past from the life between birth and death and his future up to death playing into what lives in his soul by way of feeling. Hence man's life of soul [*Gemütsleben*] is so inexplicable to himself; it appears as something elemental since as feeling it is already colored by what is still to be experienced.

All this had to be taken into consideration at the time when I wrote my *Philosophy of Freedom*. Why did I have to stress that the free deed can proceed only from pure thought? Simply because if the deed is based on the feeling, the future is already playing into it, and therefore a really free deed could never arise out of feeling. It can arise only from an impulse truly based on pure thought. If you remember what I have presented in the last two days, you will be able to see the matter still more clearly. I have said that what actually takes place in us, what goes on in our human nature, is reflected up into our consciousness in feeling. If I make a sketch, I can say that in feeling there streams upward into our consciousness just what the experience of the feeling is, but downward there streams what can be experienced by Imaginative consciousness as dream pictures (see drawing), that is, what comes into play entirely in Imaginations. For the entire human being, therefore, the life of feeling runs its course in such a way that what we are conscious of as feeling streams upward (blue), and downward there streams into the organization what is actually picture, what is really seen when it is seen through Imaginative consciousness as picture (red, inside). For the ordinary consciousness this streams down into the whole human being as something quite unknown. Not indeed in the individual events, for they must first come about—I beg you to realize this—but in the general mood of life there lives in man as a sort of basic tone the outcome of his future experiences. It is not as if the pictures of what takes place lived there; the impressions of it live in the pictures.

You must not imagine these pictures that stream downward to be like a movie reeling off the future; you must rather picture them as the result of the impressions. Only in

the case of certain people who have an atavistic clairvoyance can pictures arise that may be interpreted as pictures of definite facts, and then there can be a certain vision into the immediate future. Today, however, we shall mainly interest ourselves in the fact that what constitutes man's world of feeling descends into him in a pictorial way.

Now, as we pass over from feeling to willing, what enters man here, as I presented to you, presses outward and becomes his karma that is becoming, his future karma (red, outside). What arises in man through his feelings, therefore, has to do with his karma up to his death, while what arises out of the willing is concerned with his karma beyond death.

It is therefore fully possible to follow these things and study them in detail. As the development of anthroposophical spiritual science progresses, one never talks in an abstract way of mere concepts; one speaks rather of the concrete reality that lives in man, which, when he brings it to consciousness, can give him an explanation for the first time of what he actually is. You must receive a strong feeling, however, of how the will, depending as it does on the life of feeling, actually works into the future beyond death, how the will is the creator of future karma.

If we turn once more to the other side, to the web of thought that we found and that lives in man really between the etheric body and the physical body, we must be clear about the following. In experiencing something of the world through sense impressions and thus forming a sensory world conception, in working over these sense impressions thoughtfully, we actually weave with our subjectivity within this web of thought. What we experience in our soul as a result of the sense impressions we unite on the one hand with what is incorporated into us through birth as a web of thought. The objective web of thought, however, remains unconscious, and only that which we interweave, which we press in, as it were, out of our own inner activity of thought, enters our consciousness. It is actually as if the web of thought were there; the subjective thoughts strike against it, beat their way into this web of thought, and this web of thought then reflects our subjective thoughts in a helter-skelter way so that our subjective thoughts come into consciousness (drawing). Note that I say, in a helter-skelter way.

Let us say that you perceive some outer object, a cube, for example, a crystal cube: I will describe the exact process. First of all we see it. We do not stop short at seeing. We think about it, but the thought continues up to the web of thought, and the web of thought, which is incorporated into us through birth and which we have attached to ourselves when we were in the cosmos, which in fact we received through the cosmos—this web of thought is constituted in such a way that we now begin from certain hypotheses to form crystalline ideas that we build up out of our inner being. In forming thoughts, for example, of the isometric system, the tetragonal, the rhombic, the monoclinic, the triclinic, the hexagonal systems, that is to say, in thinking out crystal systems in a mathematical, geometrical way, we find that we can think out the crystal systems. This cube fits into the isometric system that we have cultivated in our inner being. In incorporating something such as, for example, the thought of the cube, into what are, as it were, *a priori* thoughts that we draw out of our inner being, we are, in this moment when subjective thoughts arise in us, led to the region of objective thoughts. What we cultivate as the geometric element, as purely geometrical-mechanical physics and so on, we draw out of this web of thoughts that is incorporated into us with our birth; the separate, individual elements that we incorporate into these thoughts that we develop about outer sense perceptions and impressions are those that become clear to us in letting them be reflected back to us. They must be permeated, however, by the web of thought living and forming in us eternally—the process at all events is eternal, if not in its individual forms, for these alter from incarnation to incarnation.

We live, therefore, in that we think and incorporate the thought element into our inner life of thought in such a way that we understand it; we live in such a way that we draw forth what is within this web of thought also for our subjective thinking.

Now, what I have just said is something that takes place in the human being continuously, that plays into man's life continuously. At the same time, however, you will see that if on the one hand we begin with feeling we observe what enters from feeling into the organism, what passes over into the will. What stops short in the will, as it were, remaining in the I, becomes future karma. All this brings us in the direction of man's future. If we look to the opposite side, to the web of thought toward which our subjective thoughts also flow, this brings us completely into the stream of the human past. Hence our past on this path, our completed karma, is also to be sought. In feeling, in the most essential sense, past and future meet each other in the human being. The human being is thus born, as it were, out of thoughts. He lives through feeling and weaves in his will what goes with him through the portal of death.

With these words we point to what we actually have subjectively in our life of soul between birth and death. We can go still further, however; we can turn out attention to the following. We can ask ourselves: what actually happens when the subjective thoughts, which we tie to the outer impressions, unite with what is certainly only the past, as I have just described? You see, the subjective thought becomes conscious to us first as thought. As thought it has a certain conceptual content [*Vorstellungsinhalt*]. We think a content when we think about the cube. You must be quite clear, however, about what I suggested two days ago, that in the life of soul we cannot simply separate thinking, feeling, and willing.

In willing all the motives of our moral thoughts are living. Also in thinking, however, in subjective thinking, we are conscious that not only do we have a thought content, but we link one thought to another, and we are conscious of the activity that links one thought to another. What, then, is at work in thinking? In a delicate way, the will lives in thinking, particularly in subjective thinking. We must be clear, therefore, that in thinking there lives on the one hand the content of thought and on the other hand the will's activity in thinking. Now, if the thoughts strike against us here (see drawing, page 82), they are reflected back to us, of course, as thoughts, but in the thoughts, in these subjective thoughts that we project inward, thrust inward toward the web of thought, the will in fact is also living. We cannot actually use this will in our ordinary consciousness; just think how it would be if this activity that I have pointed out to you here came quite clearly to expression in memory—in memory, the will must already have disappeared! It must still be active, but when the memory is complete, when the remembered thought is there, the memory certainly would not be pure, it would not clearly reflect what it should reflect as a past experience, if it were permeated by will! When you remember what you ate yesterday, you naturally can no longer alter the soup, for the will is already outside, is it not? The pure content of thought must arise. In reflecting, therefore, the will must be laid aside. Where does it go then?

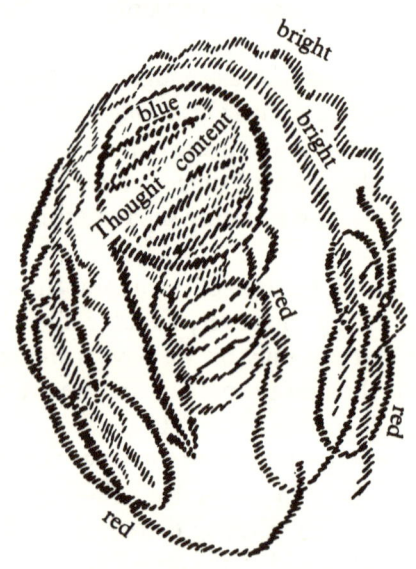

Now, if I make the same drawing and have the web of thought here, and there the reflecting, then the content of thought simply enters the consciousness. The will content of the thought goes below and unites itself with the other content of will and feeling and passes into future karma, becoming thus a constituent of future karma (light shading; dark shaded arrows from above).

On the other hand, our will impulses are like a sleeping portion even during our waking life. We do not see down below into the regions where the will actually lives. We first have the thought of the will impulse. This then passes in an unconscious way, as it were, into willing, and only when willing is manifested outwardly do we observe again what happens through us, what we experience in ordinary consciousness through willing. With deeds we actually experience everything in the conceptual life; we dream of it in the life of feeling, but we sleep over it in the actual life of will.

It is thoughts, however, that we direct into this life of will. Yes, but when? Only when we do not surrender ourselves to our instincts, our desires, to the so-called lower human nature—for this is indeed down below—which urges us then to willing and to deeds. We receive our will, however, into that which constitutes our subjective experience when we control it with our pure thoughts, which are directed toward willing, that is to say, when we control it with our intuitively grasped moral ideals. We can give these intuitively grasped moral ideas to the thought-will on the path down below toward the region of the will. In this way our will becomes permeated by our morality, and hence in the inner being of man the struggle takes place continuously between what man sends down into the will region out of his moral intuitions and what rages and boils down below in his instinctive, dreamlike life. This is all going on in the human being, but what goes on in the human being down below is at the same time that in which his human future beyond death is being prepared. This future thrusts up into the region of feeling. This future actually lives in willing. It thrusts upward into the region of feeling, and more is woven into feeling than what I have already described as the mood of feeling that has a significance for the life between birth and death. In the general state of feeling that I have described as ranging from an extreme depression to complete wildness and excess of gaiety, there can take place everything in which the human past and the human future play into one another in the life between birth and death. Also what goes beyond death, however, penetrates into what comes up from below. And what is living there? Something lives there that we sense as something objective, because it emerges out of the regions where consciousness no longer participates. It is also something objective, because it has to do with the laws by which we bear ourselves as moral beings through death. What is reflected there is the conscience. Grasped psychologically, this is the actual source of conscience. If psychology really wished to approach these things, it would have to investigate the details of the soul life along these lines, and everywhere it would find confirmation of the guiding principles given by anthroposophical spiritual science, right into the most minute details of the life of soul.

We see, therefore, that our feelings stream toward our thoughts. They stream first toward our subjective thoughts and give them life, but they also strike against the objective web of thoughts, and in this we experience ourselves as given, as beings who have come into earthly existence through birth. On the other hand, we can experience ourselves as beings who go through death. One need only study the inner being of man and one finds proclaimed in that inner being something that points beyond man, that is, beyond birth and death; it points therefore into that world which is not encompassed within the sensory, for this world that is not encompassed within the sensory indeed gives us what actually exists in our inner being. It would be of especially great importance if there were research in a *real* psychology (what is considered psychology today is nothing but a sum of formalisms) into the mood of soul of the human being in a moment where past and future flow into one another. Much that is enigmatic in human life would be discovered in this way, and people would be convinced that a protest very easily made has, in fact, no basis. The protest that is often made is this: well, what would a man become if he were continually examining himself and gazing into his inner being in order to see from his subjective mood of soul what perhaps lay in his future? This protest is easily made, but it is only fanciful. It is imagined that the way in which the future appears is just the same as it is when actually beheld and experienced. The future is not reflected, however, as it is later experienced! It is experienced in intercourse with the outer world, in encounter with things in the outer world. What goes on inwardly in man manifests itself as a raying out and is something that can never mislead him on his life's path, however precisely he knows the human being. Generally, the protests against a knowledge of the human being arise out of fear based utterly on illusions, which one creates because one judges simply by the life of ordinary consciousness, because people will not rise to the view that as soon as consciousness ascends into higher regions it experiences something entirely new.

Yesterday I showed you how, when man comes through the portal of death, he develops himself with two longings that proceed on the one hand from the life of thought and on the other from the life of will. We saw how the thought life longs for cosmic existence and how the will life after death longs for human existence. This lasts until what I called the Midnight Hour of Existence, when a rhythmic reversal then takes place. The thought element then begins to long for the human state, and the will element begins to long to pour itself out into the cosmos. The will element thus lives in the inherited characteristics, while the element of thought lives in the individual, in what is incorporated into the new earthly life.

The will element surrounds us, as it were, in what we receive from our ancestors, seen outwardly in the inherited characteristics and inherited substances. The thought element is that which is incorporated into us, and during life we again unite this thought life with all that we draw up from the depths of the life of feeling and will. This thought life at first is incorporated into us not as something warm and living like our inner life generally. Were we to remain with the thought life as it was when we were born, we would become thought automatons, as it were, full of inner coldness. At the moment of birth, however, the individual inner being begins to stir out of the will and out of the feeling and to permeate with warmth and life that which had first become cold on the way from death to birth. Hence as human beings we have the possibility of permeating with individual warmth that which must constitute cold in us out of the wide universe.

Man thus incorporates himself into the spatial and into the course of world becoming. He thus stands within it. These things are completely hidden from present-day natural scientific thinking. Present-day natural scientific thinking does not wish to approach a true knowledge of the human being. Man thus experiences himself today—and will do so always more and more—in such a way that he cannot recognize in himself his actual being, though he may recognize much about the surrounding world. By reason of the present scientific education and education in general, man lives in such a way today that fundamentally he grasps nothing of his own being. This state will increase more and more. If it could be fully realized what comes to the human being directly through one-sided natural scientific knowledge, he would be entirely estranged from himself. His inner individual element would want to live upward and to melt, through its warmth, the ice masses that we have carried into earthly existence through birth. The human being would go to pieces in his soul in this process that inwardly overpowers him; it indeed goes on without his knowledge, but he can endure it for a long period only if he recognizes it. All the signs of the times point to the fact that the human being must really come to the self-knowledge characterized. It is simply the task of the present life of spirit in its progress toward the immediate future truly to embody these things in cultural evolution.

Education, however, has employed up to now great quantities of fear, great quantities of antipathy, to prevent the vindication of what is so necessary to humanity if it does not wish to sink into decline but to come to a new ascent.

VI

Dornach, October 7, 1921

We have seen how the study of the conditions of soul of the human being leads us into the spaces, as it were, between physical body, etheric body, astral body, and I; the study of the spiritual conditions in the human being, however, leads us beyond the phenomenon of the human being as he is here in his life between birth and death out into the vast spiritual universe. One might say that insofar as the human being is spirit he stands absolutely in relation to the whole spiritual universe. Hence it is only in this connection with the entire universe that we can study what takes place in the human being as spiritual events. The soul element is, so to speak, man's intimate inner life, taking its course in a threefold form in such a way that the thinking aspect is situated between physical body and etheric body, the feeling aspect between etheric body and astral body, and the aspect of willing between astral body and the I. We therefore remain in our study of the soul element entirely within the human being. As soon as we approach the actual spiritual events, however, we must leave the human being as he usually confronts us as a self-contained being in the world between birth and death.

Now we know—and eight days ago we were speaking of this from another viewpoint—that when we first ascend into the spiritual we come to beings who are arranged above the human being in the same way as the human being has his place above the animal, plant, and mineral realms. As we ascend we therefore have—names add nothing to the matter—the angeloi or angelic beings, the archangeloi or archangelic beings, and the archai or primal beings, time spirits. We have already characterized from various points of view these beings who constitute the realm we encounter when we perceive the position of human beings in regard to the spiritual. The beings whom we designate as angeloi or angels are those who have the strongest relationship to the individual, to the single human being. The individual human being actually has a relationship to the hierarchy immediately above him such that he in a way—this is not expressed very exactly, but it can be said in the way that it is commonly expressed—develops a certain relationship to such an angelic being.

Those that then make up the second hierarchy above him are the archangels. We can say of them that among their functions is that which works as folk spirit, that which therefore embraces groups of those belonging together as a people, although here there are all possible gradations.

When finally we ascend higher, to the archai, we have the guiding beings throughout certain epochs of time, beyond the differentiations among peoples. These are certainly not the only functions, let us say, of these beings, but to begin with we receive certain conceptions if we keep to these particular functions that they perform.

Just as we can make man's physical life on earth comprehensible by asking ourselves what kind of relationship the human being has to the animal organization, to the plant organization, and to the mineral organization, so we must also ask ourselves, in order to learn what man is as a spiritual being, what kind of relationship he has to these ascending stages of beings in the spiritual.

For this we must proceed in the following way. Let us picture from certain viewpoints the way in which the human being goes through the portal of death. We know that in this age of earthly evolution that encompasses many years we live as human beings in such a way that there are present in the ordinary consciousness the laws underlying the mineral realm. From birth to death man fills himself, we might say, with everything that makes the mineral realm in a certain sense comprehensible, and he has a feeling that with the concepts and ideas at his disposal he is able to understand the mineral realm.

It is not the same where the plant realm is concerned. You know that science stops short on coming to the plant realm; at best it holds to the ideal that the complicated combination of the plant cells, of living cells generally, will one day be explicable in their structure. As I have explained to you, this is beginning completely at the wrong end, because the structure of the plant, or of living cells generally, is not distinguished by being a particularly complicated structure but by the chemical structure passing into chaos. Man, however, does not get beyond the concepts of the mineral realm. With his mineral concepts he comes still less—if I may venture to say so—to what concerns the animal realm or even to self-knowledge. All this must be given by spiritual-scientific investigations. The human being thus adopts a mineral consciousness, let us call it, that is, a consciousness adapted to the mineral realm. The human being carries the outcome of this consciousness, the weaving of which takes place between birth and death, with him through death. When he therefore goes through the portal of death and lives in the spiritual realm itself, he can journey through his further existence with what became of this consciousness.

There is essentially something else, however, that pushes up into this consciousness. What penetrates up into this mineral consciousness, in spite of not belonging to it, what colors it, is the moral consciousness. This is what arises out of all the processes of consciousness connected to our will impulses, to our conduct. What we feel as satisfaction about this or that, what we feel as remorse, as reproach and the like, all this gives color, as it were, to our mineral consciousness and is something that the human being takes with him through the portal of death. One can therefore say that the human being goes through the portal of death with a mineral consciousness colored by moral experience; with what becomes of this consciousness, he then lives further in the spiritual realm.

Man not only understands the mineral world through this mineral consciousness, but through this mineral consciousness he develops his relationship to the being from the hierarchy of the angels, therefore to that being to whom he wishes to turn as the nearest to his individual development. When the human being has gone through the portal of death, it is a question of how far, through the consequences of his mineral consciousness, he can preserve intact his relationship to this angel being. He can do this only in accordance with what from the moral side has colored this mineral consciousness, for after death this mineral consciousness strives, as it were, to spread itself out in the world. It strives to become cosmic, to adapt itself to the whole universe; it strives to get beyond what is individual.

We can also say that in life between birth and death man is nearest to the angel being when he is living in the condition out of which dreams arise, which certainly also have something to do with his individual being, and which on the one hand deny and on the other hand hold fast to this mineral-thought being. Man would be unable to find even the subconscious relationship to the hierarchy of the angels were not this mineral consciousness colored by the conditions that in a certain sense he sleeps through but that reach up out of the sleeping condition and live out their life in the world of dreams. The dream itself, although in its outlines it does not adhere to outer sense reality and often actually denies contact with it, is nevertheless woven out of the same substance as the world of thoughts is woven between birth and death. In going through the portal of death, therefore, in order to maintain the relationship to his angel being, the human being takes with him what he has developed in himself within his mineral consciousness.

Now in the way we live today in humanity's present epoch man—especially when he reckons himself to be among the most enlightened—penetrates but little with his moral experience into what he possesses as mineral consciousness. On the contrary, he makes every possible effort to hold this mineral consciousness quite apart from the moral sphere. He would like at least to set up these two worlds; on the one hand he would like to study what ultimately may be comprehended in the realm of mineral nature, and the mineral nature in the plant, animal, and human realms, and would then like to study the moral element as something surging up from his inner being. It is not harmonious with the spirit of the time to think of what lives in nature as being at the same time permeated with moral impulses. There yawns an abyss between what is of a moral and what is of a mineral nature. The human being does not easily find the bridge to incorporate the moral into the mineral nature. I have often drawn attention to how man pictures the evolution of the earth to be a purely mineral affair, from the content of the Kant-Laplace theory up to the mineral nature of modern thinking, and how man eliminates everything in the way of moral feeling. It thus comes about that the human being is able to develop only an extremely slight relationship to the being of the angeloi; in our present age he cannot unite himself intimately with his angel being, to use an ordinary expression.

If the mineral consciousness were completely separated from moral coloring, then at what I call the Midnight Hour of Existence man would face the danger of entirely losing the necessary connection with his angel being. I say he would face the danger. Today only a small number of people face this danger, but if a spiritual deepening of the whole evolution of humanity on earth does not come about, a deepening of human thinking, human feeling, and human willing, then what lives as a danger may be realized. Then there would be countless human beings who, on approaching the Midnight Hour of Existence between death and a new birth, would have to sever the relationship to their angel beings. It is true that the angel being would always keep the relationship on his part, but it would remain one-sided, from his side to the human being. The human being between death and a new birth would not be able to reciprocate adequately. We must be perfectly clear that in our modern civilization, hastening as it is toward materialism, the human being injures his relationship to his angel being, so that this relationship becomes ever looser.

Just when the human being is approaching the Midnight Hour of Existence, however, he must enter into relationship to the archangelic beings through the angel being. Should this relationship be of such a nature—as it may well be when man is living in the spiritual world—that it not only comes from the side of the angel being to humanity but can be reciprocated by the human being, then man must absorb a spiritual content, which means that he must color his moral impulses religiously.

If the present trend of evolution persists, the human being of today faces the danger of his connection with the angel being becoming so slight that he cannot form any inner relationship to the archangelic being. The archangel, however, participates in bringing man back into physical life. This archangelic being is particularly involved in building up the forces that bring man back into the community of a certain people.

When human beings live inwardly unspiritually—as has been the case for centuries—the relationship of the archangel to the human beings develops one-sidedly, and then man does not grow into his people with the inner soul being, but he is inscribed from outside, as it were, by means of the world order, into the people that the archangel is assigned to guide. One does not arrive at an understanding of our present age, which may be characterized by the one-sided way in which the peoples are cultivated, until one knows that this actually may be attributed to the souls who have recently come down to earthly existence having a loose relationship to their angel beings and by reason of this having no inner relationship to the archangelic being—thus growing into their people only from without. The people thus remains in them as an impulse from outside, and it is only through outer impulses that human beings take their place within a people, through all sorts of impulses inclining toward chauvinism. He who stands within his people with soul—and this is the case with very few people today—will be unable to develop in the direction of chauvinism, of one-sided nationalism; he takes up the fruitful forces within the people and develops these, makes these individual. He will not boast of his people in a one-sided way. He will let his people flow into his being as color, as it were, flow into his human manifestations, but will not parade this outwardly, and particularly not in an outwardly hostile attitude toward others.

The fact that today it is exactly this that provides the keynote for world politics—that all relations built on peoples create such difficulties today for human evolution—all this rests entirely on what I have been indicating. If the bond that begins in the Midnight Hour of Existence—before and after this, throughout long periods—cannot be ensouled by one's taking the appropriate religious inwardness through the portal of death—a religious feeling that is spiritual and not merely a matter of lip service—then the archangel is able to work only on what is plant-like in the cosmos and what as plant-like nature is imparted to the human being. Through very subconscious forces connected with his plant nature, which means with that which is placed in him by his breathing condition and is modified by all that has to do with conditions of language, by everything, therefore, that in language pushes in a plant-like way into the human organism, through all this man can be guided only by his archangel. It then happens that when the human being is born, when he grows as a child, he grows into his language in a more-or-less outer way. Had he been able to find the relationship, the inner relationship of soul, to his archangel through his angel, he would then have grown with his soul into all that had to do with his language, he would have understood the genius of the language, not merely what constitutes the outer mechanical aspect of it.

Today, however, we can see how strongly it is the case that in many respects the human being is an imprint of the mechanical in his language, so that actually he does not bear the element of language as a keynote in his entire being but receives an exact imprint of it. One can see quite clearly how the facial expression itself is an expression of the element of language. What confronts us in the people, what confronts us as their unique, national physiognomy, comes to man from the archangels in a completely outer way.

What takes place outwardly in humanity, insofar as it works into the spiritual of the human being, actually can be explained only through the kind of study we pursue in an anthroposophical spiritual science. All modern anthropology and things of that kind are actually what might be called a mere playing with terminology. In what is written today by anthropologists or their kind about the configuration of humanity on the earth, about the differentiation of humanity, we really in many respects have nothing to orient us, no guiding viewpoint, because what is there understood as concept is merely the classification of outer characteristics. One could just as well redistribute the whole picture. A real content streams into the matter only if it is studied spiritually. Then, however, one must not shrink back if in this study real, concrete spiritual beings arise.

One sees from this that only spiritual deepening can heal

the damages of our modern age. The damages of today, insofar as they confront us in public life, are founded on the loose relationship of the human being to his angel and the consequent loose bond with the archangel, who is thus able to have an influence only from outside.

When a human being between death and a new birth undergoes his further evolution, which after the Midnight Hour of Existence leads him once more into physical, earthly life, he enters especially the realm of the archai, of the primal spirits. These archai, these primal spirits, in the present cosmic evolution have to do with leading the human being back into the earthly limits of his being.

When the human being passes through the portal of death his further life takes its course in such a way that he experiences to begin with the consequences of his mineral consciousness with its moral coloring—thereby expanding himself, as it were, over the world. Then, after the Midnight Hour of Existence, he draws himself together again. First he is led over into the plant element, which is incorporated into him. The more nearly he approaches earthly life, the more he draws himself together, so that he is able to be born once more as a being enclosed in his skin.

What must happen to a human being when he enters the realm of the archai is an incorporating, a densification, of the plant element into the animal element. In passing through the Midnight Hour of Existence, a man acquires first the forces—naturally not the organs but first the forces—which determine his breathing and also the differentiated breathing. The concentration of these forces into the actual forces of the organs comes about only after the Midnight Hour of Existence, comes about only in the realm of the archai. Man becomes, so to speak, ever more and more human. The fact is, however, that this cosmic activity exercised upon the human being as forces coming from the archai actually organizes him in such a way that the organs tend toward the animal structure. If we perceive the human being in his relationship to the cosmos we find that while the human being is striving away from the Midnight Hour of Existence toward a new life on earth he is subject to cosmic laws, just as here on earth he is subject to earthly laws. We may say the following: the human being is defined from the immeasurable expanses of the universe, in that he draws himself together more and more. Up to the Midnight Hour of Existence there is, as it were, an expansion of man, by means of his mineral consciousness, into the breadths of the universe (see drawing, arrows), into the immeasurable breadth of the universe. When the Midnight Hour of Existence arrives (see drawing, blue) those forces incorporate themselves into the human being that work in him as plant-like forces. Man returns from this Midnight Hour of Existence in order to confine himself within the appropriate limits for earthly life (arrows going in). This Midnight Hour of Existence is altogether a tremendously significant moment in human evolution.

While after his death a human being lives on into the cosmos, he becomes increasingly one with the world. He hardly distinguishes himself from the world. Expressing myself figuratively—naturally out in the cosmos we cannot speak of physical organs, but you will understand me if I

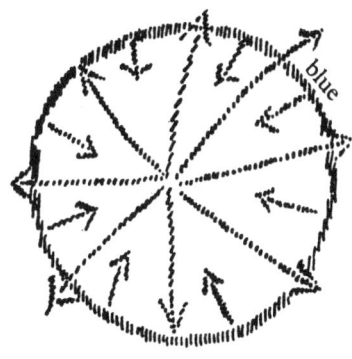

present this to you in images taken from physical existence—I might say: man learns, as it were, how the eye grows together with the light and then no longer distinguishes the eye from the light, or the sound from the ear. By expanding himself out into the cosmic breadths he grows together with the universe.

Having passed the Midnight Hour of Existence, where he begins to draw himself together in order to become once more a being with limits, there dawns in him a kind of objective conception: this is not the world, this is the human being. A consciousness grows more and more intense in the human being—a consciousness that is most intense when the human being returns into earthly life. As here on earth, however, the content of our consciousness is the minerals, the plants, the animals, the mountains, rivers, clouds, the stars, sun, and moon, so on our way back to the earth the being of man is the main conception.

It is really so that if we take the seemingly quite complicated world that lies outside our skin, with all that is within it, if we take the world with its soul and spiritual elements, it is indeed most complicated; what lies within our skin, however, is just as complicated and is different from the world outside only in size, but the size is not important. Between birth and death our world is what lies outside our skin; what is within we cannot really observe except in what during life man certainly is not, namely, the corpse. From the Midnight Hour of Existence, however, until the next life on earth, the human world, the inner being of man, is his body, soul, and spirit (see drawing, right, blue). There man is, as it were, the world. Up to the Midnight Hour of Existence we gradually lose the world as we know it through the mineral consciousness; we lose it by living into the world as though it were our self, our whole, all-embracing self, so that we no longer distinguish between our self and the world. In returning, our world becomes the human being. We do not behold the stars, we behold the membering of the human limbs; we do not behold all that is contained in the universe, let us say, between stars and earth, we behold what is within the human organization, insofar as it is formed out of spirit and soul. We behold the human being, and what we thus behold is what leads us to our renewed existence on earth. We behold the human being receiving his form.

In the time of the Midnight Hour of Existence we live in the human being who is forming himself in accordance with the plant-like. When we come into the region of the archai we live in what forms the organs of the human being, in the sense of animal forces. I have said that just as between birth and death we are dependent on what works on us from the earth, so we are dependent, in that we are outside in the universe, on what is beyond the earthly—it is no longer a question of space, but naturally we can only present this in spatial terms. The moment we pass through the archai, we can express the laws that work in us in the sense of the universe—in the same way as during our life here in an earthly community we test the laws of the earth by the laws of modern physics—we can express these laws by relating ourselves to Aries, Taurus, Gemini, Cancer, Leo, Virgo, Libra, and so on.

By relating the positions of the sun to these stars, to the heaven of the fixed stars in general, in the constellations of the sun with this heaven of fixed stars we have the laws that prevail in the realm of the will of the archai. The will that prevails there, which permeates these laws, is the will of the archai.

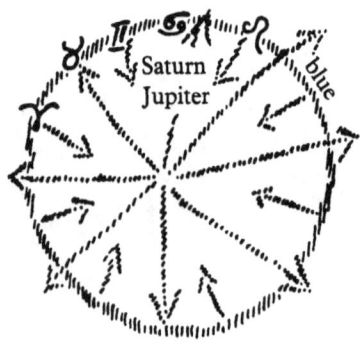

If we were to look outside for natural laws corresponding to our natural laws, as natural laws correspond to us here on earth during earthly existence, we would have to look to these constellations of the stars. We remain a long time in the kingdom where we are dependent on the star constellations—though not more dependent than we are dependent here on earth on natural laws where our will works also, which is something higher than the laws of nature. There too we may not speak of the cosmos in the sense of a cosmic law that works with mechanical necessity. What we find in the constellations of the stars, however, is the expression, as it were, the image, of these laws that work upon us there. As formerly, when we were in the kingdom of the archangeloi, the laws of the plant-like worked upon us, so now there work upon us the laws holding good in the animal realms.

When these things are found again through spiritual science, one comes upon the tremendously significant fact that the people in ancient times who used to acquire knowledge from certain dreamlike visions of the universe, which were then lost, that these people really showed a touch of atavistic genius, one could say, in naming this picture circle, which represented for them the heaven of the fixed stars, the Zodiac (*Tierkreis*, "animal circle"). I can only think that our new science of the spirit, which shows us these things again, is led from a completely different basis to an understanding of what was once grasped in a dimly sensed knowledge. It is tremendously moving when one finds the teaching about the Zodiac and its influence on the human being preserved from ancient times and when one then—quite apart from what has been preserved—with the means at the disposal of present-day spiritual science, comes once more to connect knowledge with the constellations of the sun, with the zodiacal signs, in other words, with the heaven of the fixed stars.

It is this that links the more recent science of the spirit so closely to the wisdom of the ancients. Between our time, when we wish to make spiritual science our quest, and this period when the wisdom of the ancients held sway, we have an age that was indeed necessary for the striving after human freedom; this age basically, however, was an age of darkness.

We thus come into the realm of the archai and receive and incorporate into us that which is our animal nature. What is our animal nature? Our animal nature is above all what gives us our organs, which even in number are very similar to the organs of the higher animals. Before we approach birth, however, we are stripped—if I may so express it—of the realm of the Zodiac and enter the realm of the planets—Saturn, Jupiter, and so on. In entering the realm of the planets, and thus in coming nearer to the earth, nearer the point of time when we take on the boundaries of our human form, what is incorporated into us out of cosmic law as the animal nature is given its direction, if I may express it in this way. Before we sink down into the planetary system, and therefore into the forces of the planetary system, our vertebral column, for example, has not taken on a direction away from the earth, which would raise the head aloft. We are more subject to the directional forces governing the posture of the animal. Everything, for example, that designs the hands as the organ of our soul element, not only as an organ for grasping or for walking—what makes of them organs that can act freely out of the impulses of the soul element, all this we owe to this planetary influence. All that helps us to be truly human, right into the lowest stages of our animal organization, we have by virtue of the constellations of the moon with the rest of the planets.

We are made human, therefore, as we return through the planetary system. I told you that man himself, man as he forms himself, is the world that is living in our consciousness during our return journey from the Midnight Hour of Existence. We also see how at first everything is present in him that ultimately pulsates in rhythm with the animal forces. We live through this in such a way that we actually experience a kind of decline, a kind of icy process. All this, however, is loosened on our entering the planetary realm, and this first forms the cosmic world, which we see as the human world, the world represented by the earthly human being who wrests himself away from the animal element, who grows out of the animal element. All this now fills us; it becomes the content of our consciousness. We carry in us as a system of forces that which the cosmos has given us.

Thus we descend soul-spiritually from the spiritual worlds. We have lived through the worlds in which we were in direct touch, stood in connection with, angels, archangels, archai. We descend as man. It is true, however, that if, in the way characterized, we have failed to establish an intimate relationship to our angel being, we have difficulties when penetrating into the planetary region, because we have been unable to make any divine-spiritual connection with the world of the archai. Outwardly we become incorporated into a people. The archai are then obliged to work into us, as it were, only from outside. Through this we are given a definite place on the earth, for all the forces of the archai tend toward that end. The archangels give us our place among a people and our particular place within this people is then determined by the archai. Not imbued with soul and spirit, however, we grow in an outer, mechanical way into this environment.

This is a characterization of our modern age—that the human being no longer has that inner relationship, that intimate inner relationship, that he had to his environment in more ancient times, when he grew into this immediate environment also with his soul. This is still maintained at best in a caricaturish way—as a caricature, I repeat—when today, even if it is already coming to an end, children perhaps grow up in some particular castle after previously having been attracted to their ancestors. Here we will have a relationship that in earlier ages had to do with the soul element. Today a human being is pressed into his environment in such a way that he basically has little inner relationship to the place in which he finds himself, to which his karma takes him in an entirely outer way, so that he feels his whole placement into physical existence as something external to him.

When man's being is formed through education and life in such a way that he is filled with soul, filled with spirit, and comes to a spiritual conception of the world, he will then carry this through life between death and a new birth so that he does not lose the inner connection with his angel, so that through his archangel his soul is carried into his particular people, and so that he is not placed in a merely outer way into his immediate existence by the world of the archai. He should rather be able to absorb once again into his animal organization something that he experiences in such a way that he says: there is a deep significance in the fact that just from this place where my consciousness first gradually awakens, where my education is carried on—that just from this place I am to unfold my activity in the world. This is certainly something that should lead us to bring about reform in education, so that the human being once more feels that from the place where he is educated he takes something with him that gives him his mission in the world. When this is so, a human being grows beyond the merely outer realm of the archai. He will experience the forces directing human beings in a way that is permeated by soul and spirit, and he will grow into his new life in a way different from what is frequently the case today.

What happens, then, when the human being enters a new earthly life? His consciousness is filled with the way in which he is building himself up from within as a human being. He is filled with a world that he beholds, a world of activity, not a mere world of thought. As I have already mentioned, after the Midnight Hour of Existence this world gradually takes on the tendency of the will toward being human, and the human being immerses himself into what is offered him through heredity in the generations, through the substance he receives from his ancestors. Into this he immerses himself. He envelops himself with the physical sheath; he enters the physical world. On observing the human being spiritually, we can actually find out about the content of the soul element when he is immersing himself in a new life in physical existence.

Of all the realms lived through by the human being between death and a new birth it is natural that a human being comes into the closest relationship to the angeloi, archangeloi, archai, but these things stand in further relationship to the higher hierarchies. Between death and a new birth a human being thus pursues his course through a realm in which his relationship to that realm depends on what he carries through the portal of death. The extent to which he has succeeded in permeating with his mineral consciousness that which as spirit wishes to rise out of the depths of his being determines to what extent he can become intimate with his angel being. By being able to be intimate in this way with his angel being, however, he grows into the world of the archangeloi, so that knowing, as it were, experiencing their forces out of himself, he can consciously reciprocate and proceed further, so as to become the individualized being he must gradually become if the world is to move toward its ascent and not its decline.

It is perfectly possible to give from the most varied points of view a deeply significant description of this life between death and a new birth. One point of view is to be found in the lecture course I held in 1914 at Vienna;[7] today I have been developing another point of view for you. All these points of view are intended to lead to increasing knowledge of the human being from his spiritual aspect. Those who are unwilling to explore a whole spiritual world in this way will never be able to grasp the spiritual in man himself. Just as we must go into the spaces between physical body, etheric body, astral body, and I in order to penetrate the soul element in its objective nature, so we must proceed out of the human being into the spiritual world to study his relationship to this spiritual world. Then we discover what actually weaves and lives in the human being as the spiritual. It is only the love of comfort today that makes man speak of the spirit in general terms. We must become capable of speaking about the spirit in all its particulars, just as we do of nature. Then there will arise a real human knowledge; as man needs it, the primeval saying of truth will be fulfilled, the saying that sheds its light from ancient Greece, the fulfillment of which must continue to be striven for by the human being—the truthful saying, "Know thyself."

Self-knowledge is knowledge of the world, and world knowledge is knowledge of self, for if we are living between birth and death, the stars, the sun, the moon, mountains, valleys, rivers, and the plants, animals, and minerals are our world, and what lives within our human boundaries is what we are. If we are living between death and a new birth, then we are what is concealed as the spiritual behind sun, moon, and stars, behind mountains and rivers, and our outer world is then the inner being of man. World and man alternate rhythmically, the human being living both physically and spiritually. For the human being here on earth the world is what is outside. For the human being between death and a new birth the world is what is within. Hence it is a question only of alternating through the times for man to be able to say that, in the most real sense, knowledge of man is knowledge of the world; knowledge of the world is knowledge of man.

VII

Dornach, October 8, 1921

Our recent studies have led us to consider the relationship of the human being to the spiritual world, and this relationship has in its turn made it necessary for us to cast a glance at the development man goes through between death and a new birth. We will take this as our starting point today.

Yesterday we said that the human being carries through the portal of death what I called a mineral consciousness. It can be called this because essentially its content is the mineral world with its laws, and this consciousness therefore is tinged by, or rather steeped with man's moral feelings and experiences. Bearing with him what comes from these two directions, the human being makes his way in the world through which he journeys between death and a new birth. When we consider what the human being is after death, we find that the astral body and the I have wrested themselves free from what surrounded them as a kind of shell, that is, from the physical body and the etheric body.

Now, if we picture the cosmic evolution of humanity, together with the cosmic planetary bodies that have to do with it, we know, from the description given in my *Occult Science*, how in the past this cosmic evolution has gone through the Saturn, Sun, and Moon evolutions, and how the human being then arrived at the Earth evolution, in which he is still involved. We also know that essentially in the Saturn evolution the first rudiments of the physical body were formed as a kind of universal sense organ that was developed further in the Sun, Moon, and Earth evolutions. We know that the first rudiments of the etheric body were added during the Sun evolution, those of the astral body during the Moon evolution, and that the Earth evolution is actually the time during which the I of man is evolved.

When we consider the human being as a whole, we find that he has his ego through the bond of the human being with the earth, for through those forces that exist on earth the I is formed, is molded. If we now say, therefore, that the human being passes through the portal of death, bearing his I through it, he really takes through the portal of death all that he has from his earthly evolution, all that he acquires within the earthly evolution. We bear through the portal of death just what belongs to the earthly evolution, and it is during the earthly evolution that the mineral world has been added to the other kingdoms. This, too, you may gather from my *Occult Science*. The outer, mineral world is, therefore, bound up with the evolution of the I. That the I goes through the portal of death with a mineral consciousness is essentially connected with what the human being actually has gained from the earth.

If we comprehend the earth only in a general way, however, as it first appears to us as world body, we understand it very imperfectly. The earth as world body, as it were, is a being that may be compared to a large drop in the infinite ocean of space; but this drop is constituted in such a way that it is differentiated in its substance—it contains substances of varying weight, varying density. We need only observe the metals in the earth to find that they are of varying density. What the human being incorporates into himself from the earth with the mineral consciousness originates from the whole earth, and it originates simply because the earth is a complete planet in the cosmos. What is differentiated into the various mineral substances then works in such a way that the human being takes with him through the portal of death not only what his I has become but also, for a time, what was his astral body. This has been described in my books, *Occult Science* and *Theosophy*, as the passage of the human being through the soul world.

We may therefore say that when the human being leaves the earth he develops the mineral consciousness. At first, however, this consciousness is permeated with all that the human being takes with him from the differentiated earth, from the earth insofar as it consists of various substances. This constitutes the period of his passage through the soul world. We can therefore say that the human being takes with him something that then goes on further and that to begin with is not only his I but is in a certain way an astral fruit of the earth (see drawing, page 119).

If we then follow the human being further, after he has laid aside this astral fruit of the earth, as described in my book, *Theosophy*—where it is shown how a short time after death man completes his passage through the soul world—we find that his I goes on further. At first, however, it is permeated by mineral consciousness. When we raise our spiritual gaze to where the human being is, we find the mineral consciousness of the deceased human being, that is, the thought world, which is related to what is mineral. It is actually the case that this thought world borne by man through death works on earth, and also in the cosmos, upon what is the mineral kingdom (see drawing, page 119).

This is an extraordinarily noteworthy and significant relationship. When we look at our minerals here on earth, when we observe the mineral kingdom that is also in the clouds—for there, too, there are mineral effects—and ask ourselves what spiritual essences are at work there, we must answer that in these mineral formations, which show us their outer side when as human beings on earth we observe them with our physical senses—in all these mineral effects live the thoughts to which human thought comes after death. If we look at the mineral kingdom intelligently, allowing our gaze to peruse this mineral kingdom, we can say that in all this mineral activity there is working inwardly that which constitutes the consciousness of the dead at the beginning of their career beyond the earth. We must therefore—and not merely for outer reasons—call the mineral kingdom a non-living, dead kingdom: but we must also call it a dead kingdom in the sense that at first the human thoughts, the actual human thoughts that man harbors immediately after death, work into this mineral kingdom.

When the human being then continues his journey, he comes ever nearer the Midnight Hour of Existence. Both before and after this time he develops, in the sense in which I spoke yesterday, a consciousness that is more plant-like in nature; it is not the mineral consciousness he possessed before but a consciousness that arises through the human entity being permeated with plant-creating forces. The human being receives from realms beyond the earth something different from what the earth as such can give him; in addition to what the earth can give him, he receives what is a kind of higher consciousness, and it can become apparent to us that he develops a plant-like consciousness. During this time he works on the plant realm both on earth and in the cosmos (see drawing, page 119).

It is one of the secrets of existence that when we study the plant covering of the earth, all the vegetable existence, we are shown only its outer side; it also has an inner side. Naturally we must seek this inner side, not under the roots but above the blossoms. When we picture to ourselves the blossoming plant, we see its inner aspect in what inclines astrally toward the plants, in what lives astrally, as it were, and has its outer expression in the plant covering, in the processes of fructification, in all, therefore, that is unseen. It may be said that if one observes the plant itself purely from root to flower, the inner side would be that which is over the flower. If, therefore, we consider what can be perceived outwardly of the vegetation as an outer side, then the inner side consists of the sphere of those forces that in part have their point of origin in the consciousness of human beings in the middle period of their existence between death and a new birth—before and after the Midnight Hour of Existence. We therefore must look upon the vegetation of the earth as being connected in its cosmic existence with the whole of human evolution.

If we can say regarding the mineral kingdom that in this dead kingdom live the weaving thoughts of human beings in the first half of their life between death and a new birth, then we must say that in the vegetation of the earth is outwardly revealed what lives inwardly in the universe, so that it constitutes the world of human consciousness in the middle period between death and a new birth.

The intimate relationship between the human being and the world about which we spoke yesterday made it possible to close yesterday's study with the words, "Knowledge of the world is knowledge of man, and knowledge of man is knowledge of the world." This relationship reveals itself here in a quite special way. It shows us that here on earth we actually behold something of what the human being is between death and a new birth. If we look at the minerals, they reveal to us in a kind of outer picture what human beings do in an inwardly conscious way in the period immediately following death. When we look at the plant world, we see revealed what man does inwardly in the middle period of his evolution between death and a new birth.

To an unprejudiced view such things can be observed in a certain outer way. Whenever we consider Goethe's very peculiar nature—which is only an outstanding example—each time we are surprised afresh. What constitutes the peculiarity of Goethe's nature? For one thing, Goethe attempted again and again to become a draughtsman or painter. He never accomplished this, but the drawings and paintings he left are striking in their sureness of touch. When one considers Goethe's poems, especially some that are unusually characteristic in this respect, one says to oneself that though Goethe could not become a painter his poems are expressed in a kind of displaced painting. In his poems Goethe does a good deal of painting. If this were to be expressed in the same way as some modern talented critics do, for example, one might say (though I do not think that it is such a good thing to do) that Goethe had the tendency to become a bad painter; he carried his painting tendency into his poetry and therefore became in that way merely a painterly poet.

One may say further that those people were somewhat justified who described many of Goethe's poems as being smooth and cold as marble, even "Iphigenia" and "Tasso," in a certain sense, but still more so "The Natural Daughter." Goethe offered dramatic poems in which a sculptor actually lives, and as dramatic poems they do not breathe forth the inner life that permeates the poems of Shakespeare. In a certain respect they are poems that have stopped short and are expressed in sculptural form.

Briefly, Goethe can appear as a special genius, perhaps for the very reason that he never actually came quite fully into the world. He came to the world as a painter, but never became one. He then turned to poetry but brought things to expression in a way half-painterly. He never fully mastered the art of dramatic poetry. For this he had poetic inclinations but never actually became a real dramatic poet; he stopped short of this, turned back again, and brought it to expression in a sculptural way. When one studies Goethe correctly, one becomes conscious of something that is most characteristic of him—Goethe is a human being who was never really born quite right. He produced a theory of color but was never in a true sense a physicist. He occupied himself with natural science but never completely entered into its technicalities. In short, there was actually nothing in the world into which he entered fully—he never came into the world properly.

One might go even further, considering his relationships to women. These also developed only to a certain stage, never to the point to which they develop in ordinary human beings born correctly into physical life. One could find confirmation of this everywhere, if one feels and senses these things, and if only this feeling and sensation is not limited by ordinary pedantic, commonplace ideas and obvious objections to which I need not refer here in detail. About this thesis that Goethe was not entirely born the objection naturally may be made that he was indeed born on such and such a day in Frankfurt, as may be seen in any of his biographies. Let me draw your attention, however, to a matter that calls for comment, that he arrived in the world half dead, his body absolutely black. He therefore did not enter the world robustly but in a way that was half dead.

Let us follow his life and see how he never fully arrives anywhere—how he has setbacks, even to the point of illness. Everything is like this, even the way he went about in Weimar, inapproachable in a certain respect; one could say that he never entered fully into the world. This has its origin in the fact that he brought with him an especially large portion of the plant-like consciousness that is developed in the Midnight Hour of Existence. Hence, the urge he had toward developing the metamorphosis of the plant, in which he accomplished his greatest work: this wonderful view of the plant world.

I can well imagine that it sounds unusual to speak seriously about Goethe not having come fully into the world. There are many people who prefer to speak of the outer world as a kind of maya, speaking in general, in the abstract. When we explore how the individual stages of maya are differentiated, however, it must be admitted that it is absolutely a maya if one takes Goethe completely outwardly as do Mr. Lewes or Professor Bielschowski,[8] for example. He is most definitely not like that, however; he is quite different. His nature is such that its essential origin is really discovered in the sphere that lies just in the middle of man's life between death and a new birth.

We now come to the third part of this development,

when a new incarnation, a new earthly life, is drawing near. In this period, as you may easily imagine, the human being develops a more active consciousness (see drawing, page 119, red). Outwardly he has a consciousness such as I described to you yesterday, but he works with what now lives in his consciousness—chiefly with all that develops here on earth as the animal world. At this point, however, we cannot say that when we look at the animal world outwardly this signifies only the outer side and that the inner side leads us to human thoughts or to the contents of human consciousness during the third part of his life between death and a new birth. We cannot really say this, but we can say that if we look at the animal world this animal world yields us a kind of inner aspect. The mineral and plant realms therefore show us their outer side, as it were—the plants to a lesser degree, but they may nevertheless be included. The inner side of the plant-like is presented to us, in addition to other things, by the state of consciousness of those who have passed through the portal of death and are on the way to a new earthly life. When we look at the animal realm, however, we must actually say that this gives us its inner side, its outer side being the group-souls of the animals, which ascend up to the creativity of hierarchies beyond the earthly. There in the animal realm we cannot find in the animals themselves what works out of the human being, out of human consciousness. Rather we can say that human thoughts live and weave in the animal group-souls, in what is developing in the whole world of the animal group-souls.

During this third period the human being actually lives through all the subtle and complicated configurations of the world of the animal group-souls. This is what now becomes the human world, this world of animal group-souls. Out of what he beholds there in the world of the animal group-souls, out of what passes there in and out of his consciousness, the human being builds up his own organs. He gradually draws together, as it were, what he sees there in the breadths of the world into the active beholding of his own being. Man forms his own organism—his inner organs—out of the sum total of the animal group-souls.

We might say that the human being then builds up the principal forms of his brain—of course at first as forces, not as a lump of matter, as such, but as forces—his lungs, heart, blood vessels, and so on. The human being builds up his individual organs out of the whole relationship of the animal group-beings. Thus, whereas in the first part of his supersensible life, man constructs the outer world, he now recedes more and more into himself, finally building up the individual organs of his inner organism out of the entire world of animal group-souls.

In the last stage of his becoming, the human being then enters, as I told you yesterday, the sphere of the planetary forces. This is a later stage, as it were, that the human being undergoes. After having gone through his activity in and out of the animal group-soul system, he becomes dependent on what lives in the outer world, of what lives in the movements of the planets and their constellations. Through this the etheric body of man is prepared. Man is drawn toward a new birth. His etheric body is developed. In this etheric body there now become visible the webs of thought of which I have spoken, which are to be found between the etheric body and the physical body. Man thus now weaves into his system of organs what he has worked upon more out of feeling—feeling, however, that has been thoroughly permeated by thought. Around this he then forms a web of thought. This web of thought is therefore a result of what the human being has experienced from the working of the planetary world on his being that is approaching a new birth. He thus becomes ready to enter the sheath provided for him by what is accomplished in successive generations.

What, then, is the human being who descends? Immediately after death he poured out of himself into the outer mineral world the thought element, the mineral thought element, that he took with him. By virtue of having poured out these thoughts, will impulses and feeling content gradually press upward. All this then permeates him with the content of the plant-like consciousness. The human being now begins to work with the plant realm in the outer world; then he withdraws into himself again, works out of the animal consciousness of the group-soul activity of the animals, and builds up his organs, which he then surrounds in a certain way with the sheath woven out of the substance of thought. This is what then wants to descend into physical existence.

How does this incorporation into physical existence now take place? In earlier lectures, and also again yesterday, I have pointed out that in modern science it is expected by many that someday cells will be found to have the most complicated chemical structure for which the most complicated chemical formula will be discovered. That idea, however, is completely wrong. In the cell, even in the ordinary organic cell (see drawing below, bright), the chemical cohesiveness is not stronger than in an ordinarily complicated chemical compound; on the contrary, the chemical affinities become most chaotic in the fertilized germ-cell. The fertilized germ-cell is chaos in relation to what is material, chaos that disintegrates, chaos that really disintegrates. Into this disintegrating chaos pours what I have described to you as

the human being, which was formed as I just described (lilac). What is actually physical is then formed, not through the germ itself but through the processes taking place in the mother's body between the embryo and the environment. What descends from the spiritual world is thus actually placed into the emptiness and is only then permeated with mineral substance. What we have described here is, as you may see, an absolutely transparent process.

We cannot look upon the animal consciousness as working back but must rather say that it works up into the animal group-souls (see drawing, page 119, red arrows). Then, when the human being reaches the planetary realm, he fashions man himself and incorporates himself in this way into the place prepared for him, as I have just described.

If you bear in mind the beginning and the end of life between death and a new birth, you certainly must say that things appear that can be related to one another. In what we may call the passage of the human soul through the soul world after death there arises something that still has a relationship to the earth, something that points the human being back to what is earthly. We know that then, as I have often described for you, the human being proceeds backward through his earthly life in about one-third of the time his life lasted. What he experiences in the passage through the planetary system before birth is, as it were, the polar opposite to this. Something is imparted to the human being that he brings down with him from heaven to earth. Just as he bears out into the soul world something of what is in his astral body, by means of which he lives backward through his earthly life, so he brings with him out of the cosmos something that then permeates his etheric body—something that has to do with his etheric body in the same way as what I have called the astral fruit of the earth has to do with our astral body. What he brings from the cosmos bears the same relationship to his etheric body as what he carries as astral fruit of the earth bears to his astral body.

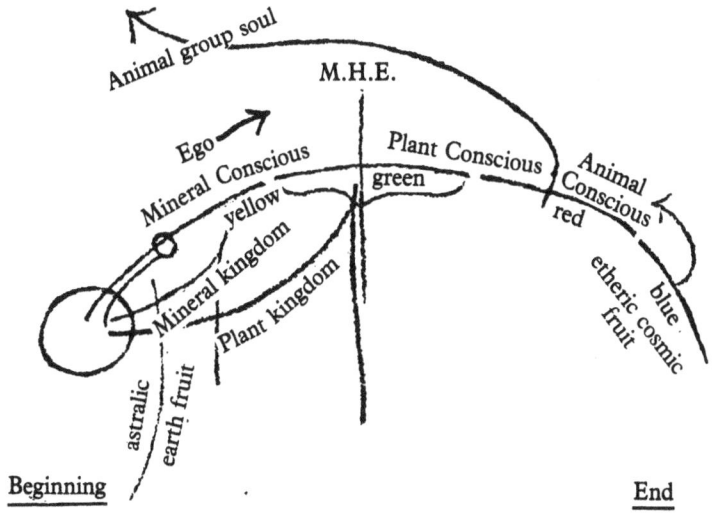

I may therefore say that the human being brings with him from the cosmos the etheric cosmic fruit. This etheric cosmic fruit actually lives on in his etheric body. From the first moment of his birth, the human being has in his etheric body something like a cosmic force impelling him forward, which works through his entire life. Karmic tendencies remaining from the past unite with this cosmic impelling force and are active in it.

We thus are able to show how perceptibly karma is related to the real human being. While telling ourselves that the human being has a pre-existent life, that he comes down from spiritual heights into earthly physical life and incorporates his I and astral body into his physical body and etheric body, we may also say that the karma he brings with him from his former life on earth incorporates itself into the etheric impelling force that he brings along with him from the influence of the planetary system that preceded his earthly incorporation.

Now you can grasp quite vividly how all that inwardly urges and impels the human being can be quite practically calculated from the planetary relationships. In this way one can look intimately into what is working in the human being and follow it out of the physical, sense activity into the soul-spiritual world, whence man again carries it down into his physical, bodily existence on earth where it continues to work. These things can be given in all their particulars.

When a person becomes filled with ideas that come from this knowledge, he will say: I enter this earthly existence in the form of physical man and am apparently shut off from the rest of the world. This consciousness of being shut off is given me where my supersensible aspect is laid into the place prepared for it by the earthly, physical existence. When I am incorporated into this sheath, however, I again grow more and more into the cosmos through my perceptions, through my experiences. I grow into it especially when I form such mental pictures of the human being's connection with the world.

Through anthroposophical spiritual science man thus learns to feel himself at one with the universe. He feels the world in himself and himself in the world. He feels the life of the macrocosm pulsing in his own inner being, and he feels how all that he inwardly experiences pulses forth again into the whole cosmos. His breathing becomes for him a symbol of all-embracing existence. The indrawn breath assumes the form of the human body and becomes inner life. The breath that leaves the organism spreads itself out again into the world. It is the same with the soul-spiritual: the whole cosmos is, as it were, breathed in soul-spiritually and becomes man. All that originates in the human being is breathed out again soul-spiritually and disperses itself in the cosmos until it reaches the very periphery of the cosmos. Then it returns once more to form the human being. In the human being we may see the image of the world, and in the world we may see the finely dissolved essence of the human being. We thus may come to an all-embracing knowledge of the world and of man in the words:

> O Man, thou art the condensed image of the world!
> O World, thou art the being of Man poured out into infinite space!

Man should acquire a consciousness that really unites his being with the cosmos, so that his future evolution may proceed in an upward, not a downward, direction.

VIII

Dornach, October 9, 1921

We have often spoken of the soul-spiritual evolution of the human being. While bearing in mind this spiritual evolution, we had to show the way in which this spiritual evolution of the human being, that is, what is spiritually active in him, arises out of his work together with the beings of the higher hierarchies, in the realms above man. If we look again into the particular nature of these higher beings, we shall be referred back to past ages of the cosmos. From my *Outline of Occult Science* we know how those beings whom we place in the realm of the angeloi, for example, went through their human stage during the evolution of the ancient Moon, how the archangeloi went through their human stage during the ancient Sun evolution, and how the archai underwent this stage during the ancient Saturn evolution. In short, if in the human being as we perceive him today we are able to understand something of the cosmos, if we wish to understand in this way these higher realms, we must look back to ages far in the past. We therefore can say that if we wish to understand the being of man as spirit, we must look up to the present evolutionary stage of beings who, in ages long past, have in their particular way gone through what the human being is going through today, during his earthly existence. To view the spiritual unfolding of the human being, we therefore must look up to higher beings as they were in the past.

We have also brought before our spiritual eyes the unfolding of the soul and have found that this soul development takes place as thinking, feeling, and willing in the spaces, as it were, between the I, astral body, etheric body, and physical body.

Now, there is no doubt that what determines man's life of soul is the present. We develop our soul by means of what we draw forth from the depths of our being. Thinking, feeling and willing develop between the four members of man's being. We take up outer impressions, work upon them, concerning ourselves in various ways with this working in the immediate present. In short, we can say that when we are considering the soul life of the human being, we must awaken an understanding in ourselves of the spiritual-soul-bodily weaving in the present.

What, then, do we find when focusing our attention on man's physical body, etheric body or body of formative forces, astral body, and I? This physical body is borne by the human being from birth, or from his life as embryo, until his death. When cast off at death this physical body cannot preserve its form. It has the possibility of preserving its form, its shape, its whole nature, only when permeated by human soul and spirit. The forces working outside in earthly, physical nature destroy it, one more quickly, another more slowly, but they destroy it. This physical body disintegrates because it cannot exist within the forces composing the earth in the mineral, plant, and animal realms. This physical body, therefore, is actually there only by virtue of the particular shape given it by the human spirit out of the higher realms, out of the spiritual realms. It is only there by virtue of the processes that the human soul carries out in connection with it in thinking, feeling, and willing. This physical body has no capacity for existence when entirely abandoned to physical existence on earth. Before a human being enters embryonic life, and after he has passed through death, what works as forces into this physical body cannot be said to belong to the earth at all. Only during the human physical, earthly life is this physical body given its form or are the corresponding processes in the physical body carried on; only then does this physical body grow, fade away, and so on. It belongs to the human being, not to the earth. This becomes clear upon simple, ordinary reflection.

Now, the moment we approach this physical world with the science of the spirit, we find that it is true that the physical body has no existence on the earth; but neither does what holds it together exist in man's conscious life. It remains entirely in the subconscious. It has, however, the nature of an inner picture, and we can grasp it if we develop Imaginative consciousness. Then we develop, as it were, the inner picture-nature of this physical body. What we behold there as the inner picture-nature offers resistance to the forces to which the substances of the physical body are unequal with their forces.

This inner picture-nature does not succumb to the earthly processes. This inner picture-nature can at least endure, and when the earth will no longer be in existence it will be carried on into the future evolutionary stages of the earth. Out of this physical human body something will then be formed that we may call a realm of nature of the future, which does not yet exist at all—a realm of nature of the future. There will arise a future realm of nature out of what today is only a picture—a realm that in its essential being will stand between our present mineral realm, which lies as though dead on the earth, and the plant realm which, immersing itself in this dead mineral realm, enlivens it, gives it life.

Imagine the mineral world, in which the plant world is immersed, participating in life—not just lying there as dead earth conveying its substances to the plants through the roots and through the air. Imagine that what the plant has immersed itself in possesses life: an entire living earth, with no dead mineral realm, and a plant world that is not merely able to immerse life into the mineral realm but is itself alive within a living mineral realm. Imagine this living mineral realm, a future stage in the metamorphosis of our earth—called in my *Outline of Occult Science* the Jupiter stage—a future, living mineral realm living in such a way that it forms itself into plants, that what now immerses itself into the plant realm in a merely material way as chemical processes will be living chemical processes, so that the plant life and the mineral shape are all one. It is this that, as future plant realm, has its seed today in the human physical body. The human physical body today is the seed of a future realm, a future realm of nature.

Let us consider man's etheric body today. During life between birth and death it remains unconscious, but it is active. Basically it is what implants actual life into us. It fills us with life. It is what contains the forces of growth and also those of nourishment. It remains in the subconscious. We cannot perceive its true form at all, but we do perceive this true form for a short time after passing through the portal of death. Then we look back on a picture-world, which is also a world of weaving thoughts. This picture-world is the true form of the etheric body. Whereas in our physical body we perceive pictures by means of our Imaginative consciousness, assuring us that in the physical body there lies the seed of a later plant-mineral realm, after death in the purely natural course of evolution our etheric body provides us with these pictures. These pictures, however, have no existence in our present earthly existence. What is in us as forces of growth, forces of nourishment—therefore all that produces our etheric, our vital existence—has no existence within the earthly. A few days after we have gone through the portal of death these pictures dissolve, and we enter a future stage of life's evolution within which we no longer have these pictures as such, as picture-etheric body, as body of formative forces. They are dissolved into the etheric cosmos, just as the physical body is dissolved into the forces of earthly existence. By means of its own being, however, this picture-existence of the etheric body shows that we have in it something seed-like, something that indeed now disappears like the seed of a plant that we conceal in the ground but that then comes up again as a plant, a formed plant. The cosmos thus absorbs our etheric body, as if dissolving it into the infinite. All that is woven in this way in the cosmos out of human etheric bodies, however, becomes in the cosmos forces of a future Jupiter realm of nature—a plant-animal, an animal-plant realm. What we observe offers us a guarantee that the human etheric body is the seed of this future realm, a realm that has its place between the world of the plants and that of the animals.

We picture to ourselves the plant world of today, which develops only life; it does not develop sensation. We picture, however, that in a substance resembling that of the present plant world but permeated by a capacity for sensation, an animal-plant realm, a plant-animal realm, develops, which will weave around the future earth, as it were, or the Jupiter planet. The sensation will not be identical with the sensation of our present animals, which is confined to the perception of the earthly; this sensation will be a cosmic sensation, a perception of the processes surrounding Jupiter.

We have here in the etheric body, therefore, the seed of a future realm, an animal-plant realm. What today is spread out around us as the mineral realm will melt away, as it were, and this will constitute the end of what is earthly. On the other hand, out of what apparently is dissolved entirely into the earthly forces, out of the human physical bodies, there will arise as seed a future world planet with its lowest realm being a mineral-plant realm. Out of what is as though dispersed after death, a second realm of this future world planet will be consolidated, an animal-plant realm, which will weave around it like a kind of living etheric activity.

As for the human astral body, we know that when the human being has passed through the portal of death he undergoes for a long time what I have described in my book, *Theosophy*, as the passage through the soul world. There I have described how in this soul world after death human experiences undergo transformations, how the human being goes through certain states that I have called burning desire, mobile sensitivity, and so on. All that is undergone there by the human being, however, even when it endures a long time, is something he also can feel as dissolving itself, even as vanishing away. Read the last few pages of this description of man's passage through the soul world after death, and, from the very way in which this is described, you will receive this feeling of disappearing in the world, that what man has been bearing in himself as astral body disappears, as if dark clouds were consumed by a universal sea of light. I have intentionally shaped the description's style so that this dissolving can be felt and sensed, as if darkness were being dissolved into the light, as if what was dead were being consumed by life. Feel how this is so in the description of the end of the passage through the human soul world after death. Then you will say that if the passage through the soul world is described in this way we have a picture similar to what appears to our spiritual eye as the imagination of the physical body, just as the human being after death has the etheric body before the eye of the soul.

If we make the description given in *Theosophy* truly living, we at once have something that in its essential nature bursts through its cocoon as seed for the future. It loosens itself from the human being, however, just as the other members of human nature are loosened from him. The physical body loosens itself to become the seed for a plant-mineral realm; the etheric body loosens itself to become the seed for an animal-plant realm. The human astral body is drawn up, as it were, by the universal world environment and becomes the seed for a human-animal realm, for a realm that raises the higher animal nature that exists today to a stage above, where the animal will not move merely in sensation, as it does today, but in thoughts, even in a certain way carrying out reasonable actions, although in a more automatic way than is the case with the present-day human being. This human-animal realm is to be pictured as one in which reasonable actions are carried out that are filled with activity from within and work outward; these actions will not, however, take the same course as those of the present-day human being, in which the reasonable action comes from the center of his I-being. Their actions will not be like that; they will have a more automatic character but will not be the same as the actions of the present animal realm, proceeding merely from instinct. They will be actions carried out by the animal, actions filled with powerful Jupiter-reason, and the single animal will be placed within this Jupiter-reason.

We now come to the human realm as such. Follow once more in my *Theosophy* how the human realm, after having shed the astral body, rises into the world of spirit and in the world of spirit has inner experiences that can be described there in such a way that the descriptions are pictures of a spiritual outer world. To be able to describe this at all, I have related how in the land of spirit something will be experienced vividly like a continental region of the land of spirit, something like an oceanic region, something like a region of air. In all that is described there in this land of spirit you have pictures of a world that does not exist for the earthly today. The present earthly environment is different. Nevertheless if we wish to describe how things actually are, this must be done by relying upon the larger, outer connections of the earthly planet—by applying to what we find in the land of spirit all that we connect with our continental regions here, and doing the same in the case of the oceanic regions. What is described as continent there, as oceanic region, as air region, as region of warmth, is seen to be permeated at the same time by what the human being carries through the portal of death as moral quality. The moral-spiritual world is described as having directly within it the outwardly substantial, the moral element there being a kind of shadowy outline that does not, however, reach the point of creating a heavenly body, a planet. What the human I lives through there, however, is the seed of these new distributions of categories, of these overall connections, on the future planet of Jupiter. In the human I today, therefore, we have the seed of what will be the overall distribution, the common life in regions that will then look different but that will be looked upon similarly to the way we look upon the regions of continents, oceans, and so on, today.

Here we are dealing with something that, in order to characterize it, to receive an idea, a concept of it, we must consider in yet another way. We must say something like this: in this weaving in the land of spirit that I have described in my book, *Theosophy*, we see at once that we are not dealing with the individual human being; in the second region, the oceanic region, we already find human beings together in human relationships, groups of human beings together; something superhuman arises. The I is lifted higher. The I joins with other I's in human groups. Read about this in my description of the land of spirit; it is something that can be described only as a realm standing above the human realm. Into such a realm the human being will enter during the Jupiter existence. It cannot be described, for instance, by my saying that it is an angel-human realm, for that would not be quite appropriate here, because when I characterize the angeloi that is a concept for the present time, which is characterized by the fact that the angels went through their human stage during the ancient Moon evolution. If I therefore wish to characterize what will develop during the future existence of the earth, or the Jupiter existence, I must speak in this way: the human being is lifted to a higher sphere; the human being in his outer manifestation, in his bodily manifestation, has developed in such a way that what today lives deep within him, only in his soul, then manifests outwardly. It might be said that just as today in a mysterious way man's inner nature is revealed by his coloring, by the color of his skin, so in the future his inner nature—whether he is good or bad—will be revealed in his outer configuration. Today we can gather only through suggestions of the human form whether a person is pedantic, irritable, cruel, or gluttonous. Certain moral qualities are expressed slightly in the physiognomy today, in a person's walk or in some outer form, but always in such a way that they can be denied, that one can plead that it is not one's fault if one has been given lips or jaws suggesting gluttony. Arguing away this outer appearance of the soul element, however, will be absolutely impossible in the future. People who cling to what is material will show it clearly in their form, they will take on Ahrimanic forms. There will be a clear distinction in the future between Ahrimanic forms and Luciferic forms. A good number of those belonging to various theosophical societies, for instance, are preparing Luciferic forms, always dreaming away in the higher regions. There will also be forms, however, that will strike the balance. The dreamy mystics, they will take on Luciferic forms; all that will be attempted through the indwelling of Christ, however, is the balance. In short, in the unfolding of what today is I-seed we will have the soul-human realm.

Seed:	Unfolding:
Human physical body	Plant-mineral realm
Human etheric body	Animal-plant realm
Human astral body	Human-animal realm
Human I	Soul-human realm

What we bear in us in our I was felt by a man who suffered tragically in the decaying civilization of the nineteenth century: Nietzsche. He felt that in order to save the future of the I, this I actually had to wrest itself away from what today is already in the midst of decline. Because the whole idea remains abstract, he has chosen the abstract word, "superman." This, however, is an indefinite, obscure urge to express what is not finished in the I but what in the I is still seed-like and as seed must point to future cosmic formations.

Nietzsche repeatedly expressed this beautifully by saying that fundamentally the human being is something that has grown out of the worm. As man has grown out of the worm, however, so the superman will grow, out of man. With this obscure feeling he associates himself with something that is the task of our age to bring to clarity, if our age does not wish to grope around in the darkness of a decaying culture, a decaying civilization.

It is perfectly comprehensible that Nietzsche, who suffered so tragically from our purely intellectual culture, should have distilled this intellectual concept of the superman, which actually has no content, out of what can be offered in the intellectual culture. Nietzsche never came to a real comprehension of the Christ, and this brought him to this peculiar situation—that out of the urge of the I-seed, and also out of the necessity to remain within the intellectual culture, he became not a worshipper of Christ but a worshipper of the Antichrist, a reverer, a glorifier of Antichrist. In Nietzsche, in a form amounting to a genius, Antichristianity appeared. This Antichristianity, however, if it were to remain what it is today, would never be able to arouse in the human being anything but dreams of an abstract superman, implanting in man at the same time the certainty that this superman dies along with earthly existence. Nietzsche wanted to cling desperately to the idea of evolution, but even this desperate clinging was no help to him. Out of the abstractions of intellectualism, he arrived merely at the "recurrence of the same," so that no higher stages could later be evolved, nothing but this repetition of the same, which, however, is only there in order to cling desperately, as I said, to the idea of evolution.

Thus we have been considering the spiritual in man, the soul element in man, the bodily in man. When we consider the spiritual in man it appears to us today as the determining spirit of the human being. When we as human spirit consider this spirit, it does not seem to us to be very differentiated. This spirit may be said to bear various hues, but it appears to us as a uniformity. To consider this human spirit in its world connections we need spiritual science. If we have not come to spiritual science, then there streams out into the world around us this undifferentiated, uniform, indefinite human spirit, and there arises a washed-out pantheism. When, however, with the help of spiritual science, we wish to learn to know this human spirit, we make our way into the world of those higher spiritual realms that stand in mutual relationship to one another and also in relationship to the human being. What we have in our spirit becomes concrete only when we find it concretely immersed in the world of the higher hierarchies. What we have in a fluctuating way within us as our life of soul, differentiated into thinking, feeling, and willing, we can only really recognize if we seek it in the stages between the various members of the human being. It is there that thinking weaves between the physical body and the etheric body, as mediator in the interaction of these two bodies; feeling weaves between the etheric body and the astral body, mediating the interbreathing of the etheric and astral bodies. When we wish to know about the life of willing, we must observe the mutual flow of forces between I and astral body, and in the interplay that develops between these two we must study the life of the will. Then we have what constitutes the present for the human being, his soul life.

When we now descend to the human corporeality, it appears to us at first as if actually destined for nothingness. The physical body, so full of significance for the human being while he lives on earth, appears, in regard to the laws of the outer realms, to be a nothing, for in them it is dissolved. They destroy it. The etheric body might be said to be held together for a short time after death, but then it is spread out in the cosmos. It vanishes from the human being; it lifts itself away from him. For the cosmos it again appears to be nothing in the present time of the earth. The astral body, at the end of his soul journey after death, is, as it were, reabsorbed from man by the soul-spiritual existence—also like a nothingness. The I is given by the earth; it seems to belong to the earth. We gain no idea at first from the I what it is destined to be in the future. If we consider these bodily members of the human being in the light of spiritual investigation, however, we discover how in the physical body, in the etheric body, in the astral body, in the I-body, there lie the seeds for cosmic worlds. The point is merely that we should discover the way to cultivate in the right way within us the seeds we bear for future cosmic worlds, so that the seeds may flourish. You know how seeds can deteriorate, and the possibility of deteriorating lies in these seeds as it does in all others.

Our bond with the Mystery of Golgotha gives us the forces that make Christ the Gardener within us. He will not allow the seeds to deteriorate but will guide them over into a future world. When the mineral realm of the earth melts away, when the plant realm of the earth withers, when the realm of the various animal species dies away, when the present form of the human being is no longer possible, because it is an emanation of the earth, belonging therefore to the earth—when everything thus disintegrates as if into nothingness, then the seeds are still there that the Gardener is guiding over into a future formation of the earthly world, called in my *Occult Science* the Jupiter world.

If we now look upon the spiritual realms above the

human being, we see them as they were in the past and understand them according to their essential being. We know that part of their present work is to bring about what is weaving and living in our spirit. If we look upon the soul world of the human being, we find the present, we find this soul world intimately bound up with the present. If we look upon man's bodily world, in this bodily world we bear in us the seeds for the future.

The bodies unveil themselves to us according to the nature of their spirituality. When we see them outwardly they are just bodies, but when we penetrate to their inner being, they are force and spirit—force and spirit, however, that grow into the future. Regarding the human being we can group past, present, and future together symbolically by saying: the past (see drawing, blue) comes in this direction, circling into our present spirituality; out of our spirituality rays forth our soul element (bright) in thinking, feeling, and willing. The thinking separates, as it were, the physical body from the etheric body; the feeling separates the etheric body from the astral body; the willing separates the astral body from the I. It may be said that everything is

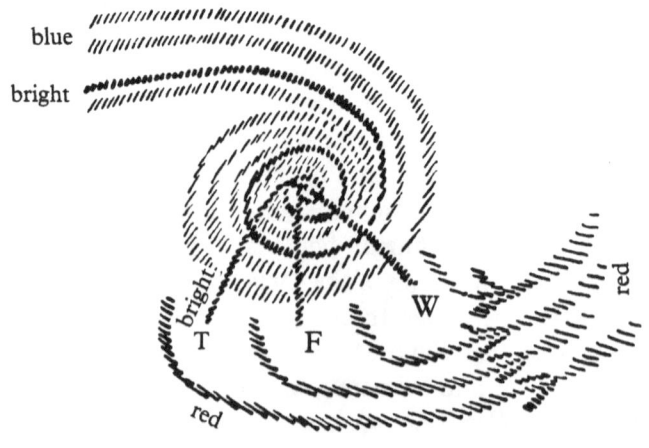

developing in a seed-like way for the future in order to form new realms (red).

We thus can put into our diagram here the various hierarchies who take an interest in us as forming part of this spiral, and we have in the picture this human vortex which as it swirls together in the center, forms the present experiences of the human being in the soul element.

It is indeed so that knowledge of the human being is knowledge of the world. This is revealed also from the viewpoint we took today. We have a world in the past. We have its effects today on the human spirit. Knowledge of the world must become knowledge of man if, out of the world, we wish to comprehend the human spirit. Knowledge of man becomes knowledge of the world in studying the bodies of the human being, if we keep in mind the essential nature of these bodies as seeds and consider how in accord with their very nature the sheathes of man today already encompass two worlds. The world of the past can be recognized in the present-day human being. Knowledge of present-day man means world knowledge of the past. Knowledge of the body of present-day man means world knowledge of the future.

Truly, from all possible points of view, world knowledge is knowledge of man. If you wish to know the world look into yourself. If you wish to know man look at the world. If you wish to know man as spirit look at the splendor of the past world. If you wish to know the splendor of the world of the future look into the seed-like nature of man's bodily present. Knowledge of man is knowledge of the world, and knowledge of the world is knowledge of man.

IX

Dornach, October 14, 1921

In our recent studies I have shown how the human being can find a relationship to the world, a relationship that he is seeking to the spiritual, the soul, and the bodily. I have also shown you that if we seriously wish to bring the spiritual nature of the human being into our consciousness, we can only apply our gaze to the spiritual worlds. For, in fact, playing into our human spirit are the deeds and reciprocal relationships of those hierarchies that we group together as the hierarchies of the angeloi, archangeloi, archai, and so on. By bringing the deeds and relationships of these beings to consciousness, the human being at the same time brings his own spirituality to consciousness.

In relation to the soul element, I was able to describe to you how thinking occurs between man's etheric body and physical body, how feeling occurs between man's etheric body and his astral body, and how willing occurs between the astral body and the I. Then I showed you how what man today can call his bodies must now be understood—if one wishes to bring them in their true form into consciousness—as the seed for future worlds. In fact, what will be formed in the world's future existence has its seed in the human bodies that we bear with us in life: in our physical body, which we lay aside here on the earth, but which, in being dissolved in the earthly realm, becomes seed for what the earth becomes after it has disappeared as earth; we learn to know our etheric body—for a short time, after we have passed through the portal of death, it apparently dissolves itself in the wide universe, but it becomes the seed for what the earth is to become in the future. This is also the case with our astral body and with that which is the sheath of our I. This I-sheath, however, as we have it here on earth as human beings, we received into our being only during this earthly existence.

We live today, which means that we have already been living for a long time in the intellectual age. The human being understands what surrounds him in the world in the same way as things generally are understood today, by means of the intellect, by means of intellectual knowing. Everything that the human being encounters today as culture, as civilization, is adjusted to this outer knowledge. Even when we feel, then, the feeling remains dull and dreamlike. What becomes clear to the human being in feeling is just what the world today presents from its authoritative science as an outer knowledge. Thus the human being, from the time he enters school, receives as inner soul life within our ordinary civilization only an intellectual mastery of the environment. How far, however, will this kind of intellectual mastery of the environment take us? I could also put the question this way: how deeply does this intellectual mastery of the environment penetrate into our soul life?

Let us consider a person who today enters school at six years of age, enters the kind of school in which he is brought into a relationship to the outer world only by outer methods. Let us assume that this person goes right through our higher education. He then is able to learn even more, is able to pass through the higher stages of culture and absorb all this into himself, by which means one becomes a leader of humanity in some realm today, in a spiritual respect. What does such a person, who has formed his soul life in accordance with the culture of our modern time, actually receive in his soul? He receives only what goes as far as his I. He receives no more than what goes as far as his I. He receives it, then, rayed back by those members of his human nature in which the I is certainly immersed but that are not called to do actual self-conscious activity. He receives as reflections his thoughts, his memory pictures, his feelings, and what he knows about his will impulses. Everything else he experiences is weakened, paralyzed. His soul life runs its course merely in the I, and everything that is communicated to him is communicated only to the extent that it enters his I.

What happens, then, if what we call anthroposophical spiritual science approaches a person? If this happens he should actually learn to feel something that can be expressed in the following way: he should feel a recognition of ". . . the I as a structure that strives to attain, with a power against which the force of gravity is like the breath of a snowflake, a state of being in which nothing that modern culture designates as talent plays a role. . . ."[9] A person, in approaching anthroposophical spiritual science, really should arrive at the point of being able to say: a very special demand is made on you with this anthroposophical spiritual science. You are able to understand things that you receive as ideas in your soul, which other people, who live only in today's culture, claim to be fantasies or deranged visions; you receive, therefore, what those who live in today's culture do not approach with their I-culture. They do not approach this with their I-culture. The earthly I cannot comprehend the concepts which, following one another, proceed from anthroposophy: what is related about the ancient Saturn, Sun, and Moon evolutions or about the spiritual, soul, and bodily nature of the human being. It can only be assumed that if one had a competent modern philosopher, one who has not become deranged or "clever" to the extent that he "takes Darwin for a midwife and the ape for an artist,"[10] if one takes such a competent modern philosopher he should understand that the spirit of the human being, about which he says so much —though the philosopher of today speaks only with words— can be comprehended only in connection with the higher hierarchies, that the soul of the human being can be comprehended according to thinking, feeling, and willing only if one looks between man's members, the physical body, etheric body, astral body, and I. Could you expect that such a philosopher would see in the bodily sheaths of the human beings, which he considered as fantasy, seeds for future worlds? One cannot arrive at such a view, of course, with what the modern I encompasses. If one is nevertheless able to link something from the soul life with this unusual idea—and to do this it is not necessary to be a clairvoyant oneself, but only to the research of the clairvoyant as ideas—this is done not in the I but in the astral body. The thought shadows, which one receives today in the I as a reflection of the astral body, do not strain the astral body. One can have these with the I-culture. If the astral body is here (see drawing, page 140, red) and the I here (green), then all that modern man experiences is here in the I, and his thoughts are nothing but what the astral body casts into the I as shadow images (yellow). It is not necessary to strain oneself by these. One allows the I to prevail, which has been received through the earthly organization. A person constructs a microscope, places a slide under it, followed by another slide and another, peers at them, and compares the thought shadows, making some mathematical calculations that proceed just as they are given, as shadow processes. It is thus possible to relate to the world, in relation to one's inner experience, completely passively. This passivity is then developed further by shifting this way of viewing to one's inner work, though not now in the Goethean sense. Such a person no longer likes to attend lecture courses in which he must participate actively with his thinking; he prefers lecture courses in which lots of experiments are done and, between the experiments, in the unpleasant babble by which the experiments are explained, he falls asleep. Or he even goes to the movies. There one need not be active at all.

This is truly the I-culture. It is prevailing more and more. Anthroposophical spiritual science comes along, however, and with that one cannot work in this way. A modern theologian said that he would not read the Akashic Chronicle even if it were bestowed on him in a special illustrated edition;[11] but he need not have feared that he would receive the Akashic Chronicle in a special illustrated edition, for it must be acquired in such a way that one participates in an inwardly forming way. Even if once one were really to fix in a symbolic, artistic way what is found in the Akashic Chronicle, this theologian still could not do anything with it because he primarily values the illustrations.

With anthroposophical spiritual science, one must participate inwardly, for otherwise one naturally hears only the words, which can be regarded arbitrarily as fantasy. This inner participation, however, one must learn to love. One must resolve to do this. It is uncomfortable, but it becomes noticeable, if one resolves to do it, that this activity refreshes, that it makes the human being fresher in soul and body. I know that many people raise objections concerning this becoming refreshed, but they would very much like to attain through merely passive thinking what should be attained through an active participation of the astral body in a difficult wrestling for comprehension, just as that theologian would have been most content to have the entire *Outline of Occult Science* played out for him in a movie. This is just how he uses his concepts in the essay where he speaks of a "special illustrated edition of the Akashic Chronicle."

Briefly, by means of anthroposophical spiritual science something comes into activity that is no longer merely the I but that includes the astral body. There are certainly those people who sense this when they read an anthroposophical book. As they read it they sense something; something stirs in them. Before things were disposed to move inwardly only passively, as thought shadows. Now something like an active intellect begins to stir in them. Something emerges from them as if inwardly they had lice, and then they become so nervous about this inner stirring that they say: this is unhealthy. Then they complain about the difficult things with which people in anthroposophical spiritual science are challenged. Especially those who then observe people who are noticeably affected inwardly in this way—their brothers, sisters, aunts, and uncles—complain that anthroposophy is something that makes people nervous.

What happens, however, if we now ask, what is the relationship between the I-culture, which man received first during earthly existence, and the culture that can be acquired through anthroposophical spiritual science? A simple sketch can make this clearer. Let us assume that the earth is here (see drawing, page 142, red). It would have been preceded by ancient Moon, Sun, and Saturn. Here we would have the next planet, Jupiter (green), which will be transformed from the earth after the earth has passed through its decline. On Jupiter, then, there participate intensively those members of the human being that exist now, as seed: the physical body, etheric body, and astral body; the I, however, takes part only under a certain condition. If the I takes up only what can be taken up through earthly culture, this I-consciousness ceases along with the earth; then the human being becomes an earthly I, and, as an earthly I, he ceases to exist along with the earth. He must evolve himself further in other forms.

If the human being has developed himself right into his astral body, however, if he has brought his astral body into activity, then this activity radiates back to his I. The being of man then consists of an I and astral body that are inwardly active. He does not feel—as I described it previously—as though he had lice inside but rather as if inwardly he were permeated by strong, healthy life forces, by life forces that now link him with what already proceeds from his bodily sheaths, as seed, into future metamorphoses of the earth, in order to develop himself further in these future earthly metamorphoses.

Anthroposophical spiritual science absolutely must be studied as something living. Then it gives the human being not merely a theory or a theoretical world view, but it gives the human being the life force that can guide him beyond mere earthly existence.

Especially if we take completely seriously a knowledge such as we have unfolded before our souls in the last three lectures—if we place the human being from the point of view of spirit, soul, and body within the entire evolution of the world and feel something as a result in the inner human content by which we become richer—then we incorporate into this human being something that carries him beyond earthly existence. For it could be—although this will not be the case, one hopes—that the human being, because he has become tired in the way characterized before, rejects anthroposophical spiritual science. Then the human sheath would continue to develop further, but it would be taken hold of by other beings than by the human beings entitled to it, and the human beings would sink into a lower existence than the one intended.

This is ultimately what it is that makes a few people in the present fearful about the cosmic future of the human being, that makes a few people sense that man, due to his trespasses, could be lost in the universe. Therefore still others must come whose insight extends beyond the assumption that "Darwin is a midwife and the ape a work of art," who do not merely believe that one ultimately speaks "under the guidance of standard medicine," about "weak nerves, fatigue, psychological weaknesses,"[12] and so, who do not merely come to the point of saying to themselves, "I won't write any more, for one would have to write with pinworms. I won't read anymore. Who is there to read? The ancient, honest Titans wrapped in sandwich paper?"[13]

Now, despite the infernal laughter which is welling up on every side, one must still say that those who have no faith anymore in the "Titans with Icarus wings wrapped in sandwich paper," those who see that everything that still has a germinal quality in our declining culture actually can only be "written about with pinworms," then ask themselves, what should one read, what should one concern oneself with? They should be given anthroposophical literature, despite the infernal laughter coming today from all sides, and they should receive, if at all possible, a soul remedy so that they can be relieved of the inhibitions that prevent them from receiving what the soul undoubtedly needs today.

Many people go around in the world who do not know what to do with themselves, people whose body becomes too heavy, inwardly crippled. They often must be shown in full seriousness the strengthening, health-giving impulses that lie in a real self-achievement of the thoughts, the ideas of anthroposophical spiritual science.

These things—I must say this again and again—have to be taken up with the greatest seriousness. It is necessary to have a little insight into the consequences actually imminent in our time from the direction upon which materialistic culture has entered.

May it also be felt how very necessary it is for the renewal of our culture to take place today from primal sources!

Tomorrow we shall continue.

X

Dornach, October 15, 1921

I want to look back once more at our recent observations. We have tried to get some picture of how the human life of spirit, the human soul life, and the human life of the body are to be comprehended. When we visualize the human soul life, that is, what the human being feels occurring within himself as thinking, feeling, and willing, then of course we find that the thinking component, or what we experience directly as the content of our thoughts, occurs between the physical body and the etheric body, that feeling occurs between the etheric body and the astral body, and willing between the astral body and the I. We thus see that our thoughts, insofar as we are fully conscious of them, represent only what glimmers up to us from the depths of our own being and really can give the waves of the soul life only their form. Something like shadows is cast upward from the depths of the human being, filling our consciousness and constituting the content of our thoughts.

Were we to depict the matter schematically, we could

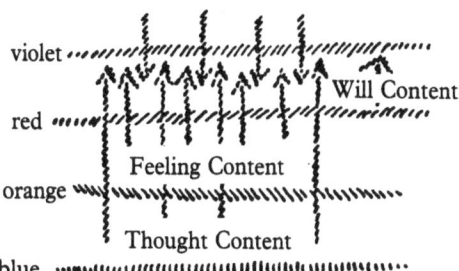

render it in this way: physical body (see diagram, blue), etheric body (orange), astral body (red), and I (violet). Then we would have the thought content between the physical body and the etheric body. From my descriptions in the last lectures, however, you have realized that this thought content in its true nature is something much more real than what we experience in consciousness. What we experience in consciousness is, as I have said, only something that generates waves from the depths of our being up to the I. They rise up to the I. The feeling content lies between the etheric body and the astral body and in turn also rises up to the I; and the will content is located between the astral body and the I. It lies the closest to the I. We can say that the I has its most immediate experience of itself in the will, while feeling content and thought content rest in the depths of our being and only send their waves lapping upward into the I.

Now we also know, however, that the content of our willing, as experienced by us, is experienced dully. Of the will, as it manifests itself in an arm movement, in a leg movement, we know as little as we do of what happens between going to sleep and awaking. The will lives in us dully, and yet it lives really within the I as the I's most immediate neighbor. If we perceive the will consciously or, let us say, in an awake manner, we do so only through the projected thought shadows that come up from the depths of our being. The mental images that we experience consciously are the shadow pictures of a deep weaving of the soul but they are still only shadow pictures, while we experience the will in a most immediate way, though dully. We can have a waking, conscious perception of the will, however, only through the shadowy thought pictures.

This is how the matter appears to us when we study our human nature while focusing in particular on the inner depths. We see, I would like to say, how little of ourselves we contain in our consciousness, how little rises upward from our inner being to our consciousness. We understand, as it were, only little of what we are like on the inside in terms of our I, and we really perceive only the hue that our thought content casts upward into this dull, will-oriented I.

With our ordinary consciousness, we can actually see as an immediate reality little more of this thought-filled, dull I than what we feel of it shortly before awakening or shortly after dropping off to sleep. It is precisely into this dull I, however, that the world of sense perceptions breaks upon awakening. Just try to become aware once of how dull your life is between going to sleep and awakening, so that you experience this dullness almost as a void. Only upon awakening, when you open your senses to the outside world, will you be in a position—thanks to your sense impressions—really to experience yourself as an I. Now the appearance [*Schein*] of the sense perceptions penetrates the I. Now the appearance of the sense perceptions fills that dull being that I have just described, so really the I lives as a fully conscious entity in the earthly human being only when we are in a state of interaction with the outside world through our sensory pictures and through all that has penetrated our senses; and coming from within as the most illuminating response we can muster is the shadowed content of our thoughts.

One can say, then, that the sense perceptions penetrate in from without. The content of our willing is perceived only dully. The feeling content rises upward and unites with the sense impressions. We see red, and it fills us with a particular feeling; we see blue, we hear the notes C-sharp or C and have an accompanying feeling. Then, however, we also reflect on what these sense impressions are. The thought content, which comes from within, interweaves itself with the sense impressions. Something from within unites with something from without. That we live in the fully awake I, however—this we actually owe to the appearance of the senses [*Sinneschein*[14]], and to this our I contributes just so much by way of response from within as I have been able to describe here.

Let us note well this appearance of the senses. Let us look upon it and realize clearly that it is entirely dependent on our physical existence. It can fill us only as we, in waking condition, put forward our physical body to meet the outer world. This appearance of the senses ceases at the moment we lay down our physical body upon passage through the portal of death, as we have already discussed in the previous studies.

Our I, then, is awakened, as it were, between birth and death through the appearance of the senses. Of our actual nature as awake, earthly human beings, we can possess only so much as is enlivened by the appearance of the senses. Imagine vividly how the being that is the human I grasps this appearance of the senses—which is, after all, only an appearance—and interweaves it with our actual human being. Now consider how there an outer becomes an inner—you can see it, for example, when you dream; consider how a delicate tissue is spun inside of us, as it were, into which the sense impressions weave. The I appropriates what comes in through the sense impressions. The outer becomes inner. Only what does become inner, however, can carry the human being through the portal of death.

It thus is only a delicate tissue to begin with that the human being carries through the portal of death. His physical body he lays down. It had mediated the sense impressions for him. Therefore the sense impressions are only appearance, for the physical body is laid aside. Only so much of the appearance as the I has taken up into itself is borne through the portal of death. The etheric body is also laid aside a short time after death. When that happens, however, our being also lays aside what is between the physical body and the etheric body. This at first dissolves, as we have seen, in the cosmos at large, constituting only the seed for further worlds, but it does not really continue to live together with our human essence after death. Only what has crested upward like waves and has combined itself with the appearance of the senses continues to live. When this is pondered, one can acquire an approximate mental image of what the human being carries through the portal of death.

Because this is so, one must answer the question, "How can someone build a connecting bridge to a departed person?" in the following way: this connecting bridge cannot be built at all if we send abstract thoughts, non-pictorial mental images over to the departed human being. If we think of the departed one with abstract mental images—what is that like? Abstract mental images retain almost nothing of the appearance of the senses; they are faded, but also there lives in them nothing of an inner reality but only what is cast up to them from the inner reality. Only a tinge of the human essence resides in mental images. Therefore, what we grasp with our intellect is in truth much less real than what fills our I in the appearance of the senses. What fills our I in the appearance of the senses makes our I awake, but this wakeful content is only interspersed with the waves that crest upward from our inner being. If we therefore direct abstract, faded thoughts to a departed person, he cannot have community with us; he can do so very well, however, if we picture to ourselves quite intimately and concretely how we stood with him on such-and-such a spot, how we talked with him, how he asked us for this or that in his particular way. The thought content, the pallid thought content, will not yield much, but it will be much more effective if we develop a fine sensitivity for the sound of his speech, for the special kind of emotion or temperament with which he held conversation with us, if we feel the living, warm togetherness along with his wishes—in short, if we picture these concrete things but in such a way that our mental images are pictures: if we see ourselves, as we stood or sat together, as we experienced the world with him. One might easily believe that it is precisely the pallid thoughts that arc across death's gap. This is not the case. The vivid pictures arc across. In pictures from the appearance of the senses, in pictures that we have only owing to the fact of our eyes and ears, our sense of touch, and so on—in such pictures there stirs something that the dead person can perceive. For at death he has laid aside everything that is only abstract, pallid, intellectual thinking. Our pictorial mental images, insofar as we have made them our own, we do take with us through death. Our science, our intellectual thinking, all of that we do not take along through death. A person may be a great mathematician, may have myriad geometrical conceptions—all this he lays aside just as he does his physical body. The person may know a great deal about the starry skies and the surface of the earth. Insofar as he has absorbed this knowledge in pallid thoughts it is laid aside at death. If, as a learned botanist, a person crosses a meadow and entertains his theoretical thoughts about the flowers of the meadow, then this is a thought content that fulfills him only here on earth. Only what strikes his eye and is colored by his love for the flowers, what is given human warmth by the union of the pallid thought with the I experience, is carried through death's portal.

It is important that one know what can be acquired here on earth as real, human property in such a way that one can carry it through the portal of death. It is important that one know how the whole of intellectualism, which has comprised the centerpiece of human civilization since the middle of the fifteenth century, is something that has significance only in earthly life and that cannot be borne through the portal of death. One thus can say: the human race has lived throughout the past ages of which we have spoken—beginning with the Atlantean catastrophe, throughout the long ages of the ancient Indian civilization, the ancient Persian civilization, through the Egyptian-Chaldean times, and then through our era up to our time—the human race has not lived in all this time, that is to say up to the first third or so of the fifteenth century, such an outspokenly intellectual life as the one we hold so dear today as our civilized life. Before the fifteenth century, however, human beings experienced much more of everything that could be borne through the portal of death. Precisely what they have become proud of since the fifteenth century, precisely what makes life worth living for the cultured, the so-called cultured, world today, is something that is obliterated upon death. One could really ask, what is the characteristic feature of modern civilization? The most characteristic feature of all, which is so praised as having been brought about through Copernicanism, through *Galileanism*, is something that must be laid aside at death, something that the human being really can acquire only through earthly life, but also something that can be only an earthly possession for him. By developing himself up to modern civilization, man has attained precisely this goal of experiencing here between birth and death all those things that have significance only for the earth. It is very important for modern man to understand thoroughly that the content of what is regarded most highly, and especially in our schools, has an actual significance only for earthly life. In our ordinary schools, we instruct our children in everything that is modern civilization, not for their immortal soul but only for their earthly existence.

Intellectualism can be grasped correctly in the following manner. When the human being awakens in the morning, the sensory pictures come streaming in to him. He notices only that the thoughts interweave these sensory pictures like a delicate net, and he is actually living in pictures. These pictures vanish immediately when he falls asleep in the evening. His thought life vanishes too, but the appearance of these sensory pictures is nevertheless essential, for he takes with him through death as much of this as his I has made its own. What comes from within—the thought content—remains, as you know, for a few days after death in the form of a brief recollection, so long as the human being still bears the etheric body. Then the etheric body dissolves itself into the far reaches of the cosmos. There is a brief experience for the human being immediately after death regarding his pictures that contain the senses' appearance, insofar as his I has made it his own: he feels these pictures interwoven then by strong lines with what he has made his own through his knowledge. He lays this brief experience aside, however, along with his etheric body, a few days after death. Then he lives into the cosmos with his pictures, and these pictures become interwoven into the cosmos in the same way in which they were interwoven into his own being before death. Before death, the pictures in the sense perceptions are formed from within. They are grasped by the human being, I might say, insofar as it is delimited by his skin. After death, after passage of the few days when one still experiences the thought life—because one still has the etheric body, before the etheric body's dissolution—after these days the pictures become in a certain way larger. They expand in such a way that they now are absorbed from without, as it were, while during earthly life they were absorbed from within. Schematically one could draw the entire process, as shown on page 153.

If this is the bodily boundary of the human being (see drawing, bright) and he has his impressions in the waking state, then his inner experiences are formed by the sense impressions within his being. After death, the human being experiences his boundary as an encompassing feeling; but his impressions wander out of him, as it were. He senses them to be in his surroundings (red). Thus a person who during earthly life could say, "My soul experiences are inside of me," now says to himself, after death, "My soul experiences

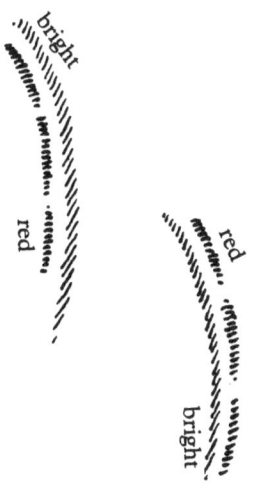

are in front of me," or, said better, "They are all around me." They merge with the surroundings. Because of this they also become inwardly different. Let us say, for example, that this person, because he loves flowers, has strongly impressed upon himself in ever-repeated sense impressions a rose, a red rose; then, when after death he experiences this wandering out, he will see the rose larger, visibly larger, but it will appear to him greenish in color. The inner content of the picture also changes. Everything that the person has perceived of nature's green, insofar as he really has experienced this green nature with human participation, not merely with abstract thoughts, now becomes for him after death a gentle reddish environment of his whole being. The inner, however, wanders out: what the person calls his inner being he will have after death in his environment outside.

These realizations, then, which concern the human being, insofar as he in turn is connected to the world itself, we can acquire through spiritual science. Only by acquiring these insights do we receive a picture of what we ourselves actually are. We cannot get a picture of what we ourselves really are if we know ourselves only as we are between birth and death, with our inwardly woven thoughts. For these are the things that as such fall away at death. Of the senses' appearance there remains only what I have just depicted to you, and it remains in the way I have described.

In the middle of the nineteenth century, when the materialistic outlook and world conception of civilized humanity had reached a culmination, as I have often emphasized, there was much talk of how the human being, when he founds a religion or when he speaks of something divine-spiritual in the outer world, really only projects his inner being to the outside. You need only read such a thoroughly materialistic writer as Feuerbach,[15] who had a strong influence on Richard Wagner, in order to recognize how this materialistic thinking sees nature as being all there is out there. That is to say, this materialistic attitude sees only the appearance of nature in the form in which it presents itself to us between birth and death and then believes that all thinking about the divine-spiritual is only the inner being of man projected outward. The result is that man feels comfortable only with the concept of the divine-spiritual as a projection of his inner being. This seeming insight received the name anthropomorphism. It was said that the human being is anthropomorphic; he pictures the world according to what lies within him. Then, of course, in the middle of the nineteenth century, the more representative among these materialistic thinkers coined a slogan that was meant to illustrate how splendidly advanced the world of human beings had now become in our modern age. They said: "The ancients believed that God created the world. We moderns, however, know that man created God; that is, God is a projection of man's inner being." They said and believed this precisely because all they knew of our inner side was what has significance between birth and death. In reality it was not just an erroneous opinion that they formed; rather, they had formed a world view that was in fact anthropomorphic, for they had no other notions of the divine-spiritual than those that the human being had managed at last to cast, to project, out of himself.

Compare with that everything that I have described, for example, in my book, *An Outline of Occult Science*. There you will not see the world described like our human mental images from within. What I describe there as Saturn, Sun, Moon, and Earth evolutions the human being does not carry within him. One must first treat what the human being experiences after death, that is, what he can place in front of himself. There is nothing anthropomorphic here. This *Occult Science* is presented cosmomorphically; that is, the impressions are such that they are actually experienced as existing outside of the human being. These things therefore cannot be understood by those people who can experience in their conceptions only what lies within the human being, as has come to be the case especially in the intellectual age since the middle of the fifteenth century. This age perceives only what resides in the inner being of man and projects it outward. Never will one be able to describe an outer world as I do in that chapter of my *Occult Science* where the Saturn evolution is treated—not even in the simplest, most elementary phenomenon—if one only projects outside what exists in the inner being of man.

You see, the human being lives, for example, in warmth. Just as he perceives the world in color through his sense of sight, so he also perceives the world in warmth through his sense of warmth. He experiences the warmth in his human inner being, I might call it, insofar as it is delimited by his skin. Already, however, he is abstracting in his perception. Warmth perceived in the life of the world really cannot be pictured otherwise than by grasping it in its totality. There is always something adhering to warmth, however, which in terms of human experience can be expressed only by referring to the sense of smell. Warmth, perceived objectively outside ourselves, always has something of scent associated with it too.

Now read the chapter in my *Occult Science* about that process of our earth that lives chiefly in warmth: where these things are described you will find simultaneous mention of scent impressions. You see from this that warmth is not described in the same way in which man experiences it in intellectualism. It is placed outside the human being, and what he experiences here between birth and death as warmth comes back after death as a scent impression.

Light is something that the human being experiences really quite abstractly here on earth. He experiences this light by surrendering to a continuous deception. I'd like to point to it here too: I have written—let me see, it must be thirty-eight years ago now—a treatise, very young and green, in which I attempted to describe how people speak of light. But where is the light anyway? Man perceives colors; those are his sense impressions. Wherever he looks: colors, he perceives some shadings of colors even when he knows it is a shade. But light—he lives in light, and yet he doesn't perceive the light; through the light he perceives colors, but the light itself he does not perceive. You may gauge the degree of the illusions in which we live in this regard in the age of intellectualism when you consider that our physics offers a "theory of light"; then we attempt to give it some substance by considering it "a theory of light." It has no substance. Only a theory of color has substance, not a theory of light.

Only the entirely healthy nature-appreciation of Goethe could suffice to create not a science of optics but a theory of color. We open our physics books nowadays and there we see light being created from scratch, as it were. Rays are constructed and reflected, and they perform all kinds of tricks. But it isn't real! One sees color. One can speak of a theory of color but not of a theory of light. One lives in light. Through the light and in the light we perceive color, but nothing of the light. No one can see the light. Imagine being in a space with light streaming through it, but there is not a single object in this space. You might as well be in the dark. In a space that is completely dark you would perceive no more than in the naked light, nor would you be able to differentiate between the two. You could differentiate only through an inner experience. As soon as a human being has gone through the portal of death, however, then, just as he perceived the scent that accompanied warmth he now perceives something about the light for which we in our present-day intellectual language do not even have an appropriate word. We would have to say: smoke [*Rauch*]; a flooding forth—he really perceives it. Hebrew still had something like that: *Ruach*. This flooding forth is perceived. That which alone could justifiably be called air is perceived there.

If we now consider what appears everywhere in our earthly circumstances as chemical reactions, we perceive them in their appearances, these chemical workings, these chemical etheric workings. Spiritually seen, without the physical body—again, therefore, after death—they provide what is the content of water.

And life itself: it is what comprises the content of the earth, of the solidity. Our entire earth is perceived from the viewpoint of the dead person as a large, living being. When we walk about here on earth, we perceive its separate entities, insofar as they are earthly entities, as being dead. On what do we base our perception of dead things at all, however? The entire earth lives, and it reveals itself immediately to us in its life if we glimpse it from the other side of death. If that is our earth, we only see a very small portion of it at any one time and are oriented to seeing just this small portion—only when we hover about it in spirit and moreover have outwardly an ability to perceive from without, so that the impressions are enlarged, do we perceive it as a whole being. Then, however, it is a living being.

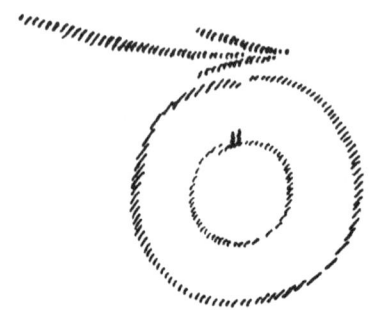

With this, I have directed your attention to something that is extraordinarily important to call to mind.

    Warmth: Scent
    Light: Smoke, Air
    Chemical workings: Water
    Life: Earth

You see, I had a conversation once with a gentleman who said that we now know, finally, thanks to the theory of relativity, that we could just as well imagine the human being to be twice as large as he really is; it's all relative, everything just depends on the human viewpoint.

This is a completely unrealistic way of looking at the matter. For let us say—the picture doesn't quite fit, but let us say—if a ladybug is crawling about on a person, it has then a particular size in relation to that person. The ladybug doesn't perceive the entire human being but, in keeping with its own size, just a small portion of the person. And so for the ladybug the person on which it is crawling about is not living but rather is just as dead to the ladybug as the earth is to the human being. You must also be able to think this thought the other way around. You must be able to say to yourself: in order to be able to experience the earth as being dead, the human being must be of a particular size upon the earth. The size of the human being is not a coincidence in relation to the earth but is completely appropriate to man's entire life upon the earth. Therefore you cannot think of man—for example, in keeping with the relativity theory—as being big or little. Only if you think and imagine quite abstractly, quite intellectually, that man is big or little; only then can you say, "If we were organized a bit differently, man might appear twice as big," and the like.

This stops when we take up a conception that goes beyond the subjective and that can keep in mind man's size in relation to the earth. After death the whole human being expands out into the universe and after a time following death man becomes much larger than the earth itself. Then he experiences it as a living being. Then he experiences chemical workings in everything that is water. In the airiness he experiences light, not light and air separately from one another but light in the air, and so on. The human being experiences, then, different pictures from those of our waking life between birth and death.

I said that we can take with us through death nothing of all that our soul has acquired in an intellectual way. Before the fifteenth century, however, man still possessed a kind of legacy from ancient times. You know, of course, that in ancient times this legacy was so great that the human being still had an atavistic clairvoyance, which then paled and dulled, withered away, and which has passed over into complete abstraction since the middle of the fifteenth century. What the human being took with him through death of this divine legacy, however, is what actually gave man his being. Just as the human being here assimilates physical matter when he enters earthly existence via birth, or rather conception, so also was it the divine essence that he brought with him and carried again through death that gave him—the expression, if I may use it at all, is unusual, but will help make this clear to you—gave him a certain spiritual weight (a polar opposite, naturally, of any physical weight). The divine essence which he brought along and took with him through death gave him a certain spiritual weight.

The way people are being incarnated now, if they are really members of civilization, they no longer have this legacy with them. At most you can still detect it here and there: those people who are not really of our civilization (and they are becoming ever fewer) still have it in them. And it is a serious matter indeed for the evolution of humanity that the human being essentially loses his being through what he acquires through intellectual civilization. He is heading toward this danger, that after death he will, to be sure, grow outward so as to have the aforementioned impressions, but he can lose his actual being, his 'I', as I have already described yesterday from a different viewpoint. There is really only one avenue of rescue for this being, for modern and future man, and it may be recognized in the following: if we wish, here in the sense world, to take hold of a reality that makes thinking so powerful that it is not merely a pale image but has inner vitality, then we can recognize such a reality issuing from within the human being only in the kind of pure thinking that I have described in my *Philosophy of Freedom* as forming the basis for action. Otherwise we have in all human consciousness only the senses' appearance. If we act freely out of pure thinking, however, such as I have described in my *Philosophy of Freedom*, if we really have in pure thinking the impulses for our actions, then we give to this otherwise "appearance" thinking, to this intellectual thinking—in that it forms the basis of our actions—a reality. And that is the one reality that we can weave purely from within out into the senses' appearance and can carry with us through death.

What, then, are we really taking with us through death? What we have experienced here between birth and death in true freedom. Those actions that correspond to the description of freedom in my *Philosophy of Freedom* form the basis for what man can carry through death in addition to the senses' appearance, transformed in the way that I have described. Thereby he regains his being. By freeing himself from being determined in the world of the senses, he regains a being after death; he is thereby a real being. If we acquire this being, it is freedom that saves us as human souls from soul-spiritual death, saves us especially for the future.

Those people who abandon themselves only to their natural forces, that is, to their instincts and drives—I have described this from a purely philosophical standpoint in my *Philosophy of Freedom*—live in something that falls away with death. They then live into the spiritual world. To be sure, their pictures are there. They would gradually have to be taken by other spiritual beings, however, if the human being did not develop himself fully along the lines of freedom so that he might again acquire a being such as he had when he still possessed his divine-spiritual legacy.

The intellectual age thus is inwardly connected with freedom. That is why I could always say: the human being had to become intellectual so that he might become free. The human being loses his spiritual being in intellectualism, for he can carry nothing of intellectualism through the portal of death. He attains freedom here through intellectualism, however, and what he thus acquires in freedom—this he can take through the portal of death.

Man may think as much as he wants in a merely intellectual way—nothing of it goes through death's portal. Only when the human being uses his thinking in order to apply it in free deeds does that amount of it that he has acquired from his experiences of freedom go with him through death's portal as soul-spiritual substance, which makes him a being and not a mere knowing. In thinking, through intellectualism, our human essence is taken from us, in order to let us work through to freedom. What we experience in freedom is in turn given back to us as human essence. Intellectualism kills us, but it also gives us life. It lets us arise once again with our being totally transformed, making us into free human beings.

Today I have presented this as it appears in terms of the human being himself. What I have thus characterized today in terms of the human being alone I shall connect tomorrow with the Mystery of Golgotha, with the Christ experience, in order to show how in death and resurrection the Christ experience can now pour into the human being as inner experience. More of this tomorrow.

XI

Dornach, October 16, 1921

Our last explorations have shown us the fundamental difference between man's whole view here, between birth and death, and in the spiritual world, between death and a new birth. We explained yesterday that in our present era, since the middle of the fifteenth century, man may gain freedom between birth and death; everything on earth that he fulfills out of the impulse of freedom gives his being in the life between death and a new birth weight, as it were, reality, existence. When we emancipate ourselves from the necessities of earthly existence, when we ascend to the point where our will is guided by free motives—that is, when our will is not founded on anything in earthly life—then we create the possibility of being an independent being also between death and a new birth. In our age this capacity to preserve our own independent existence after death is connected with something we may call the relationship to the Mystery of Golgotha. This Mystery of Golgotha may be studied from the most varied viewpoints. In the course of the past years, we have already studied a great number of these viewpoints; today we shall view the Mystery of Golgotha from the standpoint arising out of the study of the value of freedom for the human being.

Here on earth, between birth and death, the human being really does not have any view of himself in his ordinary consciousness. He cannot look into himself. It is an illusion, of course, to believe, as outer science does, that it is possible to obtain an inner knowledge of the human organization by studying what is dead in the human being, indeed sometimes by studying only the corpse. This is altogether an illusion, a deception. Here, between birth and death, the human being has only a view of the outer world. What kind of view is this, however? It is one that we have frequently called the view of "appearance" (*Schein*) and yesterday I again emphasized this strongly.

When our senses are directed toward our surroundings between birth and death, the world appears to us as appearance, as semblance. We can take this appearance into our I—being. We can, for example, preserve it in our memory, making it therefore in a certain sense our own. Insofar as it stands in front of us when we look out into the world, however, it is an appearance that manifests itself particularly—as I already explained to you yesterday—by disappearing with death and reappearing in another form; that is, it is no longer experienced in us but is experienced in front of or around us.

If, however, in the present age the human being between birth and death were not to perceive the world as appearance, if he could not perceive the appearance, he could not be free. The development of freedom is possible only in the world of appearance. I have mentioned this in my book, *The Riddle of Man (vom Menschenrätsel)*, pointing out that in reality the world that we experience may be compared with the images that look out at us from a mirror. These pictures that look out at us from a mirror cannot force us to do anything, for they are only pictures, they are appearance. Similarly man's world of perception is also appearance. The human being is not completely woven into the appearance of the world. He is woven into a world of appearance only with his perceiving, which fills his waking consciousness. If man views his impulses, instincts, passions, and temperament, and everything that surges up from the human being, without being able to bring them into clear mental images, at least into waking mental images, then all this is not appearance; it is reality, but a reality that does not rise up in man's present consciousness.

Between birth and death, the human being lives in a true world that he does not know, one that cannot ever really give him freedom. It may implant in him instincts that make him unfree; it may call forth inner necessities, but it can never enable the human being to experience freedom. Freedom can be experienced only within a world of pictures, of appearance. When we awaken we must enter a perceptive life of appearance, so that freedom can develop.

This life of appearance, which constitutes our waking life of perception, did not always exist in this way within humanity's historical evolution. If we go back into ancient times, to which we have so often looked back in our lectures, to times when there still existed a certain instinctive vision, or remnants of this instinctive vision (which lasted until the middle of the fifteenth century), we cannot say in the same sense that the human being in his waking condition was surrounded only by a world of appearance. Everything that the human being saw in his own way as the world's spiritual background spoke through the appearance. He also saw this appearance, but in a different way. For him this appearance was an expression, a manifestation, of a spiritual world. This spiritual world then vanished behind the appearance, and only the appearance remained. The essential thing in the progressive development of humanity is that in more ancient times the appearance was experienced as the manifestation of a divine-spiritual world, but the divine-spiritual vanished from this appearance, so that before man's eyes lies only appearance, in order that he might discover his freedom within this world of appearance. The human being therefore must find his freedom in a world of appearance; he does not find freedom in the true world, which completely withdrew to the dull experiences of his inner being; there, he can find only a necessity. We may therefore say that man's world of perception between birth and death—everything that I say applies only to our age—is a world of appearance. Man perceives the world, but he perceives it as appearance.

How, then, do matters stand between death and a new birth? In our last studies we suggested that after death the human being does not perceive this outer world that he sees here, between birth and death, but between death and a new birth man essentially perceives the human being himself, the inner being of man. The human being is then the world for man. What is concealed here on earth becomes manifest in the spiritual world. Between death and a new birth, man gains insight into the entire connection between the soul life and the organic life of the human being, between the activity of the single organs, and in short, everything that, symbolically speaking, lies enclosed within the human skin.

We find, however, that in the present age it is again the case that the human being cannot live in appearance after death. The life in appearance is actually valid for him only between birth and death. The human being has come to the point today that between death and a new birth he cannot live in appearance. When he passes through death, he is imprisoned, as it were, by necessity. The human being feels that he is free in his perceiving here on earth, where he may turn his eyes where he wishes; he may combine what he perceives into concepts so as to experience his freedom of action in these concepts; between death and a new birth, however, he feels unfree regarding the world of perceptions. He is overpowered, as it were, by the world. It is just as if the human being perceived in the same way as he would perceive here on earth if he were to be hypnotized by every single sense perception, if he were to be overpowered by every single sense perception so that he would be unable to liberate himself from them out of free will.

This has been the course of man's development since the middle of the fifteenth century. The divine-spiritual worlds vanished from the appearance of the earth, but between death and a new birth, these divine spiritual worlds imprison him, so that he cannot maintain his independence. I said that only if the human being really develops freedom on earth, that is, if he takes an interest with his entire being in the appearance in life, is it possible for him to carry his own being through the portal of death.

We can see what is necessary in order to develop freedom also by looking into yet another difference between the way of viewing things today and more ancient human views.

Whether we consider humanity in general or the initiates and the mysteries in ancient times, we find that the whole view of the world had another orientation from that of today. If the human being remains standing by what he has acquired since the middle of the fifteenth century, through the kind of cognition that has arisen since that time, one finds that the human being had mental images of the evolution of the earth, of the evolution of the human race; he lost track, however, of the mental images that might have given him satisfactory indications concerning the beginning and end of the earth. We might say that the human being was able to survey a certain line of evolution; he looked back historically, he looked back geologically. When he went back still further, however, he began to construct hypotheses. He imagined that the beginning of the world was a primordial mist, which appeared to be a physical formation. Out of it evolved—that is to say, not really, but people imagined that this was so—the higher beings of the realms of nature, plants, animals, and so on. In accordance with conceptions of modern physics, people thought that earthly existence disintegrates in the end (see drawing, page 172) by heat—again a hypothesis. Man thus saw only a segment, as it were, between the beginning and end of the earth. Beginning and end became a hazy, unsatisfactory picture to present-day human beings.

This was not the case in more ancient times. In ancient times people had very precise notions of the beginning and end of the earth, because they still saw the self-revelation of the divine-spiritual in the appearance. We can call to mind the Old Testament, for example, or other religious teachings of the past. In the Old Testament we find conceptions that are connected with the beginning of the world, and they are described in a form accessible to the human being, enabling him to grasp his own existence upon the earth. The Kant-Laplace nebula or primordial mist does not enable anyone to grasp human life on earth.

If you take the wonderful cosmogonies of the various pagan peoples, you will again find something that enabled man to grasp his earthly existence. The human being thus directed his gaze toward the beginning of the earth and came to conceptions that encompassed man. Conceptions of the end of the earth remained for a longer time in human consciousness. In Michelangelo's "Last Judgment," for example, and other "Last Judgments," we come across conceptions about the end of the earth, which were handed down as far as our own era and which encompass the human being; and although the ideas of sin and atonement are difficult, these conceptions do not do away with the human being.

Take the modern hypothetical conception of the end of the earth, that everything will end in a uniform heat. The entire human essence dissolves. There is no place for man in the world. In addition to the disappearance of divine-spiritual existence from the appearance of perception, the human being therefore lost, in the course of time, his conceptions of the world's beginning and end. Within these ideas he could still find his own value and see himself within the cosmos as a being connected with the beginning and end of the earth.

How did the people of past eras view history? No matter in what form they saw it, history was something that moved from the beginning to the end of the earth, receiving its meaning through the conceptions of the beginning and end of the earth. Take any of the pagan cosmologies, and they will enable you to conceive of humanity's historical development. They reach back to ages in which earthly life arises in a divine-spiritual weaving. History has a meaning. If we turn to the beginning and also the end of the earth, history has a meaning. Whereas the conception of the end of the earth, as a pictorial view contained in religious feeling, continued to exist even in more recent eras, the conception of the end of the earth lived on in historical considerations, as a kind of straggler, even in more recent times. In enlightened historical works, such as Rotteck's history of the world,[16] you may still find the influence of this conception of the earth's beginning, which gives a meaning to history. Even if only a shadow remains of this conception of the beginning of the earth in Rotteck's history, which was written at the beginning of the nineteenth century, it still gives historical development a meaning. The significant, peculiar fact is that at the same time in which the human being entered a world of perception of appearance, perceiving outer nature, therefore, as appearance, history began to lose its meaning and became inaccessible to direct human knowledge, because he no longer had any notion of the earth's beginning and end.

You must take this matter quite seriously. Take the primordial mist at the beginning of the earth's evolution, from which indefinite forms first condensed themselves, and then all the beings, ascending as far as man; and consider the death by heat at the end of the earth's evolution, in which everything perishes. In between lies what we tell about Moses, abut the great individuals of ancient China, about the great individuals of ancient India, Persia, Egypt—and further on, of Greece and Rome, as far as our present time. In thought we may add all that is still to come. All this takes place on the earth, however, like an episode, with no beginning and no end. History thus appears to have no meaning. This must be realized.

Nature may be surveyed, even if we cannot survey its inner being. It rises up before the human being as appearance in that man experiences nature between birth and death. History becomes meaningless. Man simply lacks courage enough in our time to admit that history has no meaning; it is meaningless, because man has lost track of the beginning and end of the earth. Man should really sense that humanity's historical development is the greatest of riddles. He should say to himself that this historical development has no meaning.

Individuals have had inklings of this. Read what Schopenhauer wrote on the absence of meaning in history that emerges out of occidental beliefs. You will see, then, that Schopenhauer really sensed this absence of meaning in history. We should be filled with the longing to rediscover the meaning of history in another way. Out of the world of appearance we can develop a satisfactory knowledge of nature, particularly in Goethe's sense, if we give up hypotheses and remain in the phenomenology, that is, in the teachings of appearance, of semblance. Natural science can be satisfying if we eliminate all the disturbing hypotheses about the beginning and end of the earth. We are then as it were imprisoned, however, in our earthly cave, and we do not look out of it. The Kant-Laplace theory and the end of the world by heat block our view into the distant past and the distant future.

This is basically the situation of present-day humanity from the standpoint of general consciousness; consequently humanity is threatened by a certain danger. It cannot quite enter into the mere world of phenomena, into the world of appearance. Above all it is unable to enter with the inner life into this world of appearance. Humanity wishes to submit to the necessity, the inner necessity of the instincts, drives, and passions. Today we do not see much of everything that may be realized on the basis of free impulses born out of pure thinking. Just as much, however, as the human being lacks freedom here in his life between birth and death, so he is overcome, with the hypnotizing compulsion between death and a new birth, by lack of freedom, by the necessity in perception. Man is therefore threatened by the danger of passing through the portal of death without taking with him his own being and without entering into something free regarding the world of perception, but rather into something that submerges him into a state of compulsion, which makes him grow rigid, as it were, in the outer world.

The impulse that in the future must break into the life of humanity is the appearance of the divine-spiritual to the human being in a way different from the way in which it appeared to him in ancient times. In past ages the human being could imagine a spiritual element within the physical at the beginning and end of the earth, with which he knew he was united and that did not exclude him. The human being must take up this permeation with the spiritual more and more from the center, instead of from the beginning and end. Even as in the Old Testament the beginning of the earth was looked upon as a genesis of the human being, within which his existence was ensured, even as the pagan cosmogonies spoke of humanity's evolution out of divine-spiritual existence, even as the contemplation of the end of the earth, which—as was stated—was still contained in the views of the decline of the world, which do not deprive man of his own self, so modern times must find in a right view of the Mystery of Golgotha, at the center of the earth's evolution, that which again enables the human being to find divine life and earthly life interwoven.

Man must understand in the right way how God passed through the human being with the Mystery of Golgotha. This will replace what we lost regarding the beginning and

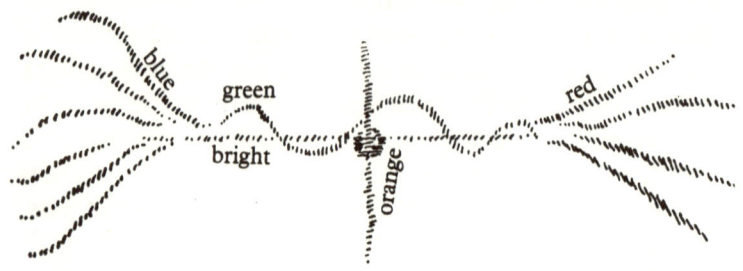

end of the earth. There is an essential difference, however, between the way in which we should now look upon the Mystery of Golgotha and the earlier way of looking at the beginning and end of the earth.

Try to penetrate into the way in which a pagan cosmogony arose. Today we often come across conceptions stating that these pagan cosmogonies were fabrications of the people. This conception holds that just as today man freely joins thought to thought and disconnects them again, so at one time people devised their cosmogonies. This, however, is an erroneous university view, which has no reasonable foundation. We find instead that in the past the human being gave himself up entirely to the contemplation of the world; he could see the beginning of the world only in the way in which it appeared to him in the cosmogony, in the myths. There was no freedom in this; it was altogether something that yielded itself to man by necessity. The human being had to look into the beginning of the earth; he could not refrain from doing so, he could do nothing else. Today we no longer picture in the right way how in the past man's soul pictured the beginning of the earth and, in a certain respect, also the end of the earth, through an instinctive knowledge.

Today it is impossible for the human soul to picture the Mystery of Golgotha in this way. This constitutes the great difference between Christianity and the ancient teachings of the gods. If the human being wishes to find Christ, he must find Him in freedom. He must freely acknowledge the Mystery of Golgotha. The content of the ancient cosmogonies was forced upon man, whereas the Mystery of Golgotha does not force itself upon him. He must approach the Mystery of Golgotha in a certain resurrection of his being, in freedom.

The human being is led to such freedom by an activity that I have recently designated in anthroposophical spiritual science as the activity of knowing. If a theologian believes that he may gain knowledge of the Akashic Chronicle in a special illustrated edition, that is to say, without needing to exert any inner activity to grasp what must appear before his soul in concepts and must become images—such a theologian would simply show that he is predisposed to grasp the world only in a pagan way, not in a Christian way; for the human being must come to Christ in inner freedom. Particularly the way in which the human being must face the Mystery of Golgotha constitutes his most intimate means of an education toward freedom.

The human being is in a certain sense torn away from the world by the Mystery of Golgotha if it is experienced rightly. What arises in that case? In the first place, the human being now can live in a world of perception, of appearance, and in this world surges up something that leads him to the spiritual existence that is guaranteed in the Mystery of Golgotha. This is one thing. The other thing, however, is that history has ceased to have meaning, because beginning and end were lost; it receives meaning again because it is given this meaning from the center. We learn to recognize how everything before the Mystery of Golgotha leads toward the Mystery of Golgotha and how everything after the Mystery of Golgotha sets out from this mystery.

History thus once more acquires meaning, whereas

otherwise it is an illusory episode without beginning and without end. The outer world of perception faces the human being as appearance for the sake of his freedom, changing history into something it should not be—an episode of appearance without any center of gravity. It dissolves into fog and mist which basically we already find theoretically in Schopenhauer's writings.

Through the inclination toward the Mystery of Golgotha, all that was once otherwise historical appearance receives inner life, historical soul, connected with everything that modern man requires through the fact that he must develop freedom in life. When he passes through the portal of death, he will have developed here the great teaching of freedom. Avowal of the Mystery of Golgotha cast into life the light that must fall on everything that is free in the human being. The human being has the possibility of saving himself from the danger that he has here by virtue of the predisposition for freedom that he has in appearance but does not develop, because he surrenders himself to instincts and drives and therefore falls prey to necessity after death. By accepting as his own a religious faith that is totally different from more ancient religious faith, in filling his entire soul only with a religious faith living in freedom, he transforms himself for the experience of freedom.

In today's civilization, basically only a small number of people have really grasped that only a knowledge gained in freedom, an active knowledge, is able to lead us to Christ, to the Mystery of Golgotha. The Bible gave man a historical account so that he might have a message of the Mystery of Golgotha for the time when he could not yet take in spiritual science.

To be sure, the Gospel will never lose its value. It will acquire an ever-greater value, but to the Gospel must be added the direct knowledge of the essence of the Mystery of Golgotha. Christ must be able to be sensed, felt, known through one's own human force, not only through the forces working out of the Gospel. This is what spiritual science strives for regarding Christianity. Spiritual science seeks to explain the Gospels, but it is not based upon the Gospels. It is able to appreciate the Gospels so fully just because it discovered afterward, as it were, all that lies concealed in them, all that has already been lost in the course of humanity's outer evolution.

The whole modern evolution of humanity is thus connected on the one hand with freedom, the appearance of perception, and on the other with the Mystery of Golgotha and the meaning of historical development. This sequence of many episodes which constitutes history as it is generally described and accepted today acquires its true significance only if the Mystery of Golgotha can be inserted into historical evolution.

Many people experienced this in the right way and they used the right images for it. They said to themselves: once upon a time, man looked out into the heavenly expanses; he saw the sun, but not the sun as we see it today. Today there are physicists who believe that out there in the universe there floats a large sphere of gaseous matter. I have frequently said that physicists would be astonished if they could build a cosmic balloon and reach the sun, for where they suppose the existence of a gaseous sphere, they would find negative space, which would transport them in a moment not only into nothingness but beyond nothingness, far beyond the sphere of nothingness. The modern materialistic cosmologies developed today are pure fantasy. In more ancient times, people did not picture the sun as a gaseous sphere floating in heavenly space; the sun in their view, was a spiritual being. Even today the sun is a spiritual being to those who contemplate the world in a real way; it is a spiritual being manifesting itself only outwardly in the way in which the eye is able to perceive the sun. This central spiritual being was experienced by a more ancient humanity as one with the Christ. When speaking of Christ, the ancients pointed to the sun. More recent humanity must now not point away from the earth but rather toward the earth when it speaks of the Christ. It must search for the sun in the Man of Golgotha.

By recognizing the sun as a spiritual being, it was possible to connect a conception worthy of the human being with the beginning and end of the earth. The conception of Jesus, in whom Christ dwelt, renders possible a conception worthy of the human being regarding the middle of the earth's evolution; from there will ray out toward beginning and end that which will once more make the whole cosmos appear in a light that gives man his place in the universe. We should therefore live toward a time in which hypotheses concerning the world's beginning and end will not be constructed on the basis of materialistic, natural scientific conceptions, but which will proceed from the knowledge of the Mystery of Golgotha. This will also enable us to survey all of cosmic evolution. In the outwardly luminous sun, the ancient human being sensed the Christ of the outer world. The true knowledge of the Mystery of Golgotha enables man to see in the historical evolution of the earth the sun of this earthly evolution through Christ. The sun shines outside in the world and also in history—it shines physically outside and spiritually in history; sun here and sun there.

This indicates the path to the Mystery of Golgotha from the viewpoint of freedom. Modern humanity must find it, if it wishes to transcend the forces of decline and enter the forces of ascent. This should be realized deeply and thoroughly. This knowledge will not be abstract, not merely theoretical, but one that fills the whole human being. It will be a knowledge that must be felt, must be experienced in feeling. The Christianity about which anthroposophy must speak will not be a looking to Christ but a being filled with Christ.

People would always like to know the difference between anthroposophy and what lived as the older theosophy. Is this difference not evident? The older theosophy has warmed up the pagan cosmologies. In the theosophical literature you will discover everywhere warmed-up pagan cosmologies, which are no longer suited to modern human beings; although theosophy speaks of the earth's beginning and end, this no longer means what it meant in the past. What is missing in these writings? The center is missing, the Mystery of Golgotha is missing throughout. It is missing to an even greater extent than in outer natural science.

Anthroposophy has a continuing cosmology that does not extinguish the Mystery of Golgotha but accepts it, so that this Mystery is contained within it. The whole evolution, reaching back as far as Saturn and forward as far as Vulcan, is seen in such a way that this light enabling us to see will ray out from the knowledge of the Mystery of Golgotha. If we but recognize this principal contrast, we shall no longer have any doubt as to the difference between the older theosophy and anthroposophy.

Particularly when so-called Christian theologians again and again lump together anthroposophy and theosophy, this is due to the fact that they do not really understand much about Christianity. It is deeply significant that Nietzsche's friend, Overbeck,[17] the truly significant theologian of Basel, wrote a book on the Christianity of modern theology, in which he tried to prove that modern theology—including Christian theology—is no longer Christian. One may therefore say that even here outer science has already drawn attention to the fact that modern Christian theology does not understand or know anything about Christianity.

One should thoroughly understand everything that is unchristian. Modern theology, in any case, is not truly Christian; it is unchristian. Yet people prefer to ignore these things due to their love of ease. They should not be ignored, however, for to the extent to which they are ignored, man will lose the possibility of inwardly experiencing Christianity. This must be experienced, for it is the opposite pole to the experience of freedom, which must emerge. Freedom must be experienced, but the experience of freedom alone would lead human beings into the abyss. Only the Mystery of Golgotha can lead humanity across this abyss.

We shall speak of this more next time.

Notes

1. Edward George Earl Bulwer-Lytton, 1803-1873.
2. "Source of destruction," *Zerstoerungsherd*; *-herd* suggests a furnace or oven as well as a source.
3. Washington Conference, a disarmament conference held from November 1921 to February 1922.
4. Jan Christiaan Smuts, 1870-1950.
5. Adolf von Harnack, church historian, 1851-1930.
6. Vladimir Soloviev, Russian philosopher, 1853-1900.
7. *Inneres Wesen des Menschen und Leben zwischen Tod und neuer Geburt*, Vienna 1914, Bibl.-Nr. 153.
8. George Henry Lewes, 1817-1878, *Life of Goethe*, 1855. Albert Bielschowski, 1847-1902, *Goethe*, 1895-1904.
9. Quotation from *Epilog*, by the German poet Gottfried Benn, 1886-1956.
10. *Ibid.*
11. Christoph Schrempf, theologian, 1860-1944.
12. Quotation from *Epilog*, by Gottfried Benn.
13. *Ibid.*
14. *Sinneschein*, appearance, semblance, illusion of the senses; literally, the shine or brilliance of the senses.
15. Ludwig Feuerbach, 1804-1872.
16. Karl Wenzeslaus Rodecker von Rotteck, historian, 1775-1840, *General History*, 1813-1818, 6 volumes.
17. Franz Overbeck, Protestant theologian, 1837-1905.

www.ingramcontent.com/pod-product-compliance
Lightning Source LLC
Chambersburg PA
CBHW031258110426
42743CB00041B/737